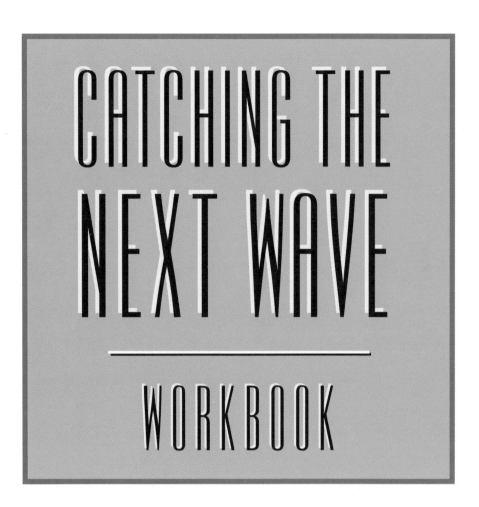

CATCHING THE NEXT WAVE

WORKBOOK

Leadership Strategies for Turn-Around Congregations

NANCY VOGEL

Augsburg

MINNEAPOLIS

ACKNOWLEDGMENTS

Thanks to:

- God for trusting me with this project.

- All the saints of Christ's church who, through diligent study, practice, and faithfulness to God's calling, have contributed to the resources that compose this workbook.

- All the members of Lutheran Ministry in Christ Church who partner with me on this journey of growing God's kingdom in a changing world.

- My colleague in ministry, Rev. Robb Grimm, for his partnership in team ministry.

- My partner in life, Fred Vogel, for his support, patience, and encouragement.

CATCHING THE NEXT WAVE WORKBOOK
Leadership Strategies for Turn-Around Congregations
Nancy Vogel

Editor: Andrea Lee Schieber
Illustrations: Marti Naughton
Inside design: Carolyn Berge
Cover design: Mike Mihelich
Cover photo: PhotoDisc, Inc. copyright © 1998

Developed in cooperation with the Division for Congregational Ministries of the Evangelical Lutheran Church in America, Marta Poling-Goldenne, project manager.

This book has a companion resource, *Catching the Next Wave: Leadership Strategies for Turn-Around Congregations*, 0-8066-3881-8. Order copies from Augsburg Fortress, 800-328-4648.

ISBN 0-8066-3882-6

Manufactured in the U.S.A.   AF 9-3882

     00   01   02   03   04   2   3   4   5   6   7   8   9   10

INTRODUCTION

If you are reading this, you probably are experiencing a negative change in your congregation and are wondering what you can do about it. You've come to the right place! This resource contains strategies for changing and building a healthy congregation. Designed to be used with the book *Catching the Next Wave: Leadership Strategies for Turn-Around Congregations*, this workbook provides the tools to get off that plateau or reverse that declining trend in health. Keep reading—your new journey has already begun.

Start by understanding that advance planning is essential. Consider a new twist to planning: "church mapping." In his book *Moving Off the Map: A Field Guide for Changing the Congregation* (Abingdon Press, 1998, p. 240), Thomas Bandy defines church mapping with the following comparisons to traditional methods of planning:

Strategic planning	➡ Ministry mapping
Linear	➡ Omni-directional
Uniform	➡ Contextual
Performed by technicians	➡ Performed by explorers
Follows a chain of command	➡ Follows individual initiative
Allows little deviation	➡ Expects constant deviation

Every congregation is called to actively embrace God's mission and vision for itself. However, the way we think, process, and respond to that call has changed. Church mapping, with its omni-directional planning, allows us to construct a system that functions with all groups and individuals going in different directions, probably all at the same time. Because one shape or size of ministry does not fit all, we must customize and contextualize our vision for ministry to match God's calling in our setting and with our strengths and gifts of the Spirit. Change happens constantly, at warp speed, with or without our participation. Therefore, once a plan is implemented, it must constantly be reevaluated and adjusted in order to seize unforeseen opportunities and meet the ever-changing needs of people.

This workbook is designed to be used by leaders in the congregation—pastor, other staff, members of the governing board. Once congregation leaders decide to engage in this process, it is critical to form a vision team. That team will also want to review and use the material in this book. As the turn-around process continues, mission task forces will also find resources here for their work.

In using this workbook, you will experience the five phases of a turn-around process: design, study, plan, act, and tend, as described in the companion book. But before beginning these phases, assess the health of your congregation. Just as the human body must be healthy to function properly, a church must be healthy to carry out God's mission. A healthy congregation is also ready to handle the Spirit-filled chaos that naturally occurs in a turn around.

If you are part of the vision team, read this entire workbook and complete the assessments. Share them with your pastor, staff member, or congregational leader. Plan together how to use this material with the congregation. As you remain one step ahead of the other people and groups in the process, you will encounter the overlap of phases and activities. Take the initiative, be an explorer, and be flexible, but never deviate from spreading the good news of Jesus Christ.

The content grid on page 5 indicates how the Bible studies, assessment tools, checklists, and other exercises can be used and reused in different phases of the process and with different groups. Each of these tools has a printed "tab" in the margin to suggest the stage(s) in which it is intended to be used.

Adapt the material to reflect the common language and concepts of your congregation.

Catching the Next Wave book and workbook do not hold every answer for you and your congregation. You, along with your pastor, church staff, governing board, congregational leadership, and members, have the remaining necessary information—it will take a team effort to make this work. In addition, there are more resources referenced in these pages for further study and reflection. Pray, trust God, and continue on this new journey.

As Christians, our mission is clear: Go and make disciples (Matthew 28:19). How we do that is usually not as clear. Once you have worked through this process, you will know what you are doing and why you are doing it, and you will put your congregation back "on the map." Let's ride the next wave with confidence—God has secured the future!

May your journey be a renewing one.

Contents

HEALTH
DESIGN
STUDY
PLAN
ACT
TEND

IS OUR CONGREGATION HEALTHY?

Seven hallmarks of a healthy congregation are described in Chapters 1–2 in *Catching the Next Wave: Leadership Strategies for Turn-Around Congregations.* They are based on understanding God's creation as a living organism with a spiritual life. Any congregation considering a turn-around process needs to start by assessing its health. But what is a healthy congregation?

The inventory on the following pages provides guidance on how to begin. It may be used at any time in the process to help people understand the concept and importance of church health.

Directions

1. Read the definitions of the hallmarks and check the characteristics that apply to your congregation.

2. Place your answers on the scoring chart that follows.

3. Individually or in small groups, use the discussion questions to process the information.

4. Keep the completed inventories to provide a benchmark for evaluating progress.

Seven Hallmarks of a Healthy Congregation

ORGANIZATION

"Life bears intrinsic organization." Every part of the structure of a living organism has a function that keeps the organism alive. For a congregation to be alive, it needs organization that is clearly defined and well coordinated.

Characteristics of a congregational system that produces ministry:

☐ Prayer permeates and connects the entire structure
☐ Spiritual gifts of staff and members are identified and used
☐ Leaders are supported and trained
☐ Volunteers are recognized
☐ Volunteers are given permission to "get the job done"
☐ A streamlined decision-making process exists
☐ Staff works in partnership with volunteers
☐ Visionary pastor(s) and staff guide organization

GROWTH

"Growth distinguishes living things from all nonliving things."

Characteristics of a congregation that is alive:

☐ Prayer-centered activities
☐ Intentional outreach into the community
☐ Positive congregational esteem
☐ Mission versus maintenance orientation
☐ Welcoming hospitality to guests at worship and other events
☐ Inclusion of new people into existing groups
☐ Creation of new groups for new people
☐ Willingness of volunteers and staff to "go the extra mile"

MOVEMENT

"Movement generates energy and momentum. As individuals and as the gathered people of God, we are moving toward God's ultimate fulfillment of God's kingdom."

Characteristics of a congregation on the move:

- [ ] People living God's call, revealed through prayer, every day
- [ ] People want to grow spiritually and numerically and to find out how
- [ ] Fervent spirituality
- [ ] A clear statement of mission and vision
- [ ] A clear sense of strengths
- [ ] A collective and individual faith that is willing to try new ways of sharing the good news
- [ ] A view that sees mistakes as learning opportunities, not failures
- [ ] Actions that address needs in the wider community

TRANSFORMATION

"Healthy organisms metabolize; that is, they transform complex chemical and physical matter for use within the body. Healthy congregations serve the gospel by being communities where faith transforms individual members."

Characteristics of a transforming congregation:

- [ ] Prayer-strengthened commitment
- [ ] Preaching of the gospel
- [ ] Administering of the Sacraments
- [ ] Learning opportunities for all ages
- [ ] Opportunities for service
- [ ] Opportunities for sharing the faith
- [ ] Loving and caring relationships
- [ ] Spiritual retreats and enrichment events

SENSITIVITY

Biologists use the term *irritability* to describe "an organism's sensitivity to stimulation in its immediate surroundings." A congregation needs the ability to sense change and challenge and be ready to deal with the issues that can threaten to upset it.

Characteristics of a congregation that is sensitive to its surroundings:

- [ ] Receives guidance and awakening through prayer
- [ ] Openly identifies and faces conflict, rumor, and gossip
- [ ] Welcomes change when it supports ministry
- [ ] Evaluates programs for effectiveness, not longevity or tradition
- [ ] Respects different opinions and perspectives
- [ ] Celebrates a variety of cultures
- [ ] Welcomes diversity
- [ ] Bridges generational gaps

Prayer

Prayer is central to congregational health. Take a look at the prayer life of your congregation. Are you seeking God's will in all you do?

- [ ] We pray at the beginning of meetings as well as at the end.
- [ ] We pray during meetings when a need to refocus arise.
- [ ] We use corporate prayer in worship and at meetings.
- [ ] We use free-form prayer in worship and at meetings.
- [ ] We have prayer groups, prayer trees, or prayer chains.
- [ ] There is prayer in classes for youth and adults.
- [ ] People are comfortable asking for prayer support.
- [ ] Prayer is seen as a gift and a tool.

Circle the number of boxes you checked to determine your prayer score.

Prayer score

1 2 3 4 5 6 7 8

Discussion questions

- ✔ What is my personal prayer life like?
- ✔ How is prayer ministry active in our congregation?
- ✔ What do we do to encourage personal prayer? Group prayer?
- ✔ How can we as individuals and as a congregation improve our prayer life?

ADAPTATION

"Life adapts. The congregation as a living entity must also adapt to its context in order to retain its relevance."

Characteristics of a congregation that adapts:
- ☐ Prays to seek new ways to serve God
- ☐ Regularly reviews community demographics
- ☐ Celebrates new people in the community, and supports them through new outreach ministries
- ☐ Incorporates new styles of music in worship
- ☐ Uses visitor-friendly language
- ☐ Uses visitor-friendly worship styles
- ☐ Allows for spontaneity with flexible organizational structures
- ☐ Employs staff members who move beyond job descriptions to make ministry happen

REPRODUCTION

"One of the most basic principles in biology is that living things come from other living things." The church is called to reproduce faith.

Characteristics of a congregation that reproduces:
- ☐ People of all ages are encouraged and taught to pray
- ☐ Intentional faith development for children and youth
- ☐ Leadership development for each new generation
- ☐ Small groups that meet human needs
- ☐ Multiplication of small groups
- ☐ Seminars and programs that reach unchurched people
- ☐ Active missionary support and work
- ☐ Daughter/satellite churches

Scoring

These seven hallmarks of health provide guidelines to evaluate the health of your congregation. Use the following scale to check the pulse of your congregation. Count the number of checks you have in each category and circle the corresponding number. Use these results to assess your overall evaluation of the health of your congregation. Remember, no congregation gets a perfect score.

Organization	1	2	3	4	5	6	7	8
Growth	1	2	3	4	5	6	7	8
Movement	1	2	3	4	5	6	7	8
Transformation	1	2	3	4	5	6	7	8
Sensitivity	1	2	3	4	5	6	7	8
Adaptation	1	2	3	4	5	6	7	8
Reproduction	1	2	3	4	5	6	7	8

Discussion questions
- ✔ What do we do well?
- ✔ What do we need to work on?
- ✔ What should be our first priority?

HEALTH

DESIGN

STUDY

PLAN

ACT

TEND

CAN THIS CONGREGATION TURN AROUND?

Unofficial estimates in the Evangelical Lutheran Church in America suggest that as many as one-third of its nearly 11,000 existing congregations are in danger of not surviving the next 10 to 15 years (*Catching the Next Wave: Leadership Strategies for Turn-Around Congregations*, p. 19).

Many factors account for this trend. George Barna cites eight symptoms of decline in congregations: demographic changes, inadequate leadership, poor management, old blood or aging membership, building campaigns or other projects that create or expose conflict, ingrown family or a focus on membership needs, resistance to change, and poor spiritual health (*Turnaround Churches*, Regal Books, 1993). In addition, the life cycle stages of birth, youth, maturity, old age, and death provide a natural downward trend when a congregation reaches maturity at 35 to 40 years old. All factors should be considered when contemplating a turn-around strategy. There may be reason to believe a turn around is not possible for your congregation at this time.

Use the following inventory to determine if there are symptoms your congregation should address before beginning a turn around. Healing old wounds, facing conflicts, or addressing negative attitudes will strengthen your congregation to turn around. Pray for God's guidance as you begin.

Directions

1. On a scale of 1 to 6 (1 is low, 6 is high), rate how your congregation faces the following challenges. Circle the corresponding number.

2. Complete the inventory individually and discuss in a small and/or large group for clarification.

3. Utilize the discussion questions to clarify information.

4. Tally information and record it for future use.

5. Determine your next step.

Attitude Check

CHANGING DEMOGRAPHICS

We know the community has changed, but we don't want to change our style, programs, or language.

We welcome cultural and ethnic diversity by creating new worship styles and programs to meet needs of new people.

1   2   3   4   5   6

POOR MANAGEMENT

Bureaucracy and hierarchy clog the decision-making process.

A spirit of permission and passion-led ministry prevails.

1   2   3   4   5   6

INADEQUATE LEADERSHIP

Leaders are very busy, but do not motivate or direct the congregation's ministries.

Leaders are visionary and inspirational, developing disciples and identifying needs in the community.

1   2   3   4   5   6

AGING MEMBERSHIP

Very few families, young adults, or children join our congregation, and the same people do all the work.

We create inviting programs and safe places for families to feel welcome and new people to connect.

1   2   3   4   5   6

MAJOR PROJECTS AND CONFLICT

Any project creates an environment for conflict.   Major projects create opportunities to work together.

1	2	3	4	5	6

FOCUS ON MEMBERSHIP NEEDS

We design our ministries to address needs of the existing members.   We design a significant number of ministries to address the needs of the community.

1	2	3	4	5	6

RESISTANCE TO CHANGE

We design ministries based on past experiences, like we have always done.   We let go of ministries that do not work and design ministries that do.

1	2	3	4	5	6

POOR SPIRITUALITY

We do not intentionally encourage study, prayer, or discernment.   We encourage and actively pursue biblical study, prayer, and discernment.

1	2	3	4	5	6

Processing the Information

Gather data from individual or small groups, then use the following questions to clarify issues:

- In what areas do we show health as a congregation?
- In what areas do we show signs of stress or conflict?
- What further discussion or research may be needed to clarify these issues?
- How will we use this information?
- What is our next step?

Evaluate the data. If you are low in any one particular area, discuss further within your own group to gain insight on this issue. Brainstorm ways in which you might be able to address this negative situation.

If you have scored less than three on four or more line graphs, you may want to consider professional intervention. Your synod staff, middle judicatory, or a private church consultant may be contacted for guidance in taking the next step. If you have scored four or more in four or more of the line graphs, continue the turn-around process. (pp. 11–12).

Determine your next step. Will you begin the turn-around process or will you seek additional help?

Suggested Resources

Your synod office or middle judicatory may have a conflict resolution team or consultant available to congregations. Outside consultants may include the following:

L.E.A.D. Consultants
P.O. Box 664
Reynoldsburg, OH 43068
(614) 864-0156
e-mail: leadinc@leadinc.com
John Savage is the founder and an active consultant with L.E.A.D. Individual consultations, seminars, and other resources are available.

Creative Consultation Services
Church Growth Center
1230 U.S. Highway Six
P.O. Box 145
Corunna, IN 46730
(800) 626-8515
e-mail: creativecs@juno.com
Kent R. Hunter is the president and director of Creative Consultation Services. Call to order an inquiry kit.

21st Century Strategies, Inc.
1126 Whispering Sands
Port Arkansas, TX 78373-5721
(512) 749-5364
e-mail: easum@aol.com
Bill Easum is founder, executive director, and senior consultant of 21st Century Strategies. A variety of resources is available, including individual consultations.

ASSESSING THE LEVEL OF CONFLICT

In addition to conducting an attitude check before engaging in the turn-around process, it is crucial to understand if conflict is present before proceeding. There are various stages of conflict; each stage has different characteristics. If your congregation is showing evidence of conflict, use the worksheet on page 12 to determine what stage of conflict is present and how best to proceed.

Evaluation Notes

For conflict stage 1 to stage 3, consider using conflict resolution tools in this workbook—"Managing Conflict in a Turn-Around Congregation" and "Managing Conflict Constructively" Bible study. When a congregation is in stage 4 moving into 5, a turn-around strategy will most likely be ineffective.

Even after seeking outside assistance or following the steps in this turn-around process to kindle the congregational vision, it is possible a turn around may not occur.

Consider These Alternatives

If a turn around doesn't seem feasible for your congregation, remember: Death is part of life. You may decide to allow the congregation to die naturally. If choosing this option, ask:
✔ Who can assist us in doing this?
✔ When might this happen?
✔ How will we help members connect to other congregations?

Work through an intentional process of closing the congregation:
✔ Can we merge with another congregation?
✔ Can we sell our assets to help plant another mission?
✔ How can we participate in that process?
✔ Can our property serve as housing to a social-ministry activity in our community?
✔ How can we help this happen?
✔ How can we turn death into life?

As members deal with the potential death of the congregation, they will pass through stages very similar to the stages of dying outlined by Elizabeth Kubler Ross in the book *Death: The Final Stage of Growth* (Prentice Hall, 1975). Consider these stages as applied to congregations:

REMEMBER
■ Pray and listen with compassion.
■ Not everyone passes through the stages at the same time.
■ Some people will move back and forth between stages.
■ Not everyone will pass through these stages in order.
■ Some may never reach the acceptance stage.

DENIAL: Members will deny that the death is happening or is necessary. They will relive the glory days and hang on to cries of victories yet to come. This is a necessary stage because it cushions the shock of the impending death.

RAGE AND ANGER: "Why this congregation?" will be a common question in this stage. Blame of themselves, each other, former management teams, middle judicatories, former and present pastor(s), and even God will surface.

BARGAINING: This stage sees people bargaining for more time. "What if we . . ." is discussed numerous times, and God hears many promises for change. However, the promises are not kept.

DEPRESSION: A calm will begin to come over the congregation as it settles into a depression. Members will begin to mourn past losses, things not done, and wrongs committed. Then "preparatory grief" begins; the end is in sight.

ACCEPTANCE: The time has come. Members now agree that the congregation will close. Feelings may include resignation, sadness, or regret. Leadership can help a congregation at this point by explaining that in death there is life. We are an Easter church!

HEALTH
DESIGN
STUDY
PLAN
ACT
TEND

Stages of Conflict

| Stage 1 | Stage 2 | Stage 3 | Stage 4 | Stage 5 |

◄ Resolve conflict and
       begin turn-around process. ►

              ◄ Seek professional assistance and
                                postpone turn around. ►

                        ◄ Consider alternatives
                                         to turn around. ►

STAGE 1:
SIGNIFICANT CONFLICT
- ☐ Significant disagreement
- ☐ Conflicting goals and needs
- ☐ Focus on problem instead of people
- ☐ Open sharing of information
- ☐ Issue clarity
- ☐ Work toward agreement using collaborative style
- ☐ Win/win final solution

STAGE 2:
MODERATE CONFLICT
- ☐ Significant disagreement
- ☐ Poorly defined issue
- ☐ Lack of trust in each other
- ☐ Withheld information
- ☐ Hostile reactions
- ☐ Focus on "saving face"
- ☐ Win/win solution with great effort

STAGE 3:
HIGH CONFLICT
- ☐ Focus on people as the enemy
- ☐ Resistance to peace efforts
- ☐ Inability to share feelings
- ☐ Distorted information
- ☐ Blame assigned to people or groups
- ☐ Rehashing of old issues
- ☐ Win/lose attitude; some people may leave the congregation

STAGE 4:
VERY HIGH CONFLICT
- ☐ Unwillingness to negotiate with others
- ☐ Focus on elimination of people
- ☐ Discussion shifts from issues to principles
- ☐ Goals driven by needs of select groups
- ☐ Individuals seeking to hurt others
- ☐ Lack of movement beyond "lines" drawn by each group
- ☐ Split within the church; significant numbers leaving

STAGE 5:
EXTREMELY HIGH CONFLICT
- ☐ Unmanageable conflict
- ☐ Vindictive language and behaviors
- ☐ Information altered to prove a point
- ☐ Individuals seeking destruction and punishment for opposition
- ☐ Highly destructive attitudes, language, and behaviors
- ☐ Removal of persons from congregation
- ☐ Possible departure of pastor; judicatory intervention required

Adapted from "Conflict Intensity Chart," © The Alban Institute, Inc. Reprinted with permission, and from "Levels of Conflict," *Effective Ministry and Membership Growth*, Evangelical Lutheran Church in America, 1996, p. 6.

HEALTH

DESIGN

STUDY

PLAN

ACT

TEND

HOW IMPORTANT ARE CONGREGATION LEADERS?

Leadership in any congregation is both a challenge to and a requirement for church health. God calls some to be leaders and others to be followers, but how do we distinguish the difference? Consider the following lists before filling any leadership position. The vision team and task forces will be responsible for leading the congregation into uncharted territory and will need special gifts and talents to accomplish that task. The following are instruments to help you identify and select the appropriate people for the tasks at hand. Remember, no one person will have all the gifts listed!

What Makes Someone a Leader?

DISCIPLINES

- [ ] Prayer
- [ ] Meditation
- [ ] Reflection
- [ ] Discernment of God's will
- [ ] Seeks new learning
- [ ] Applies new learning
- [ ] Self-care
- [ ] Family care

SKILLS

- [ ] Articulates a vision
- [ ] Enlists the support of others
- [ ] Establishes ways to turn a vision into reality
- [ ] Compromises creatively and still achieves the goal
- [ ] Deals constructively and openly with criticism/ conflict
- [ ] Uses receptive listening
- [ ] Responds positively to negative situations
- [ ] Communicates well
- [ ] Effective at conflict management
- [ ] Effective at time management
- [ ] Asks the right questions
- [ ] Anticipates the next step

CHARACTERISTICS

- [ ] Optimistic
- [ ] Positive
- [ ] Visionary
- [ ] Patient
- [ ] Resilient
- [ ] Objective
- [ ] Innovative
- [ ] Persistent
- [ ] Inspiring
- [ ] Caring
- [ ] Sensitive
- [ ] Honest
- [ ] Open
- [ ] Has a servant's heart
- [ ] Teaches by example
- [ ] Strives for excellence
- [ ] Knows own strengths/ weaknesses
- [ ] Celebrates diversity of gifts
- [ ] Willing to take risks
- [ ] "Colors outside the lines"

Questions to consider when selecting a leader:

✔ Does this person display many of the characteristics, skills, and disciplines listed here?

✔ Does this person show genuine interest and enthusiasm in this project by asking how she or he can make a difference?

✔ Does this person exhibit a heart for service rather than recognition and power?

✔ Is this person a team player?

✔ Most important, does this person display a love for Jesus Christ?

Leadership Styles

Even gifted leaders have different leadership styles. Each person will bring a gift to the leadership position in which he or she is called to serve.

MOTIVATIONAL LEADERS are leaders who are able to present new ideas in meaningful, relevant ways. They also give encouragement to people who cannot see beyond their own individual shortcomings. It is a gift to help others see the collective power of the Christian community when serving God's purpose.

VISIONARY LEADERS can see the big picture. Plans and dreams about the future become concrete and applicable to the assignment at hand and are communicated with passion and commitment. These people are positive, optimistic, and faithful.

TASK LEADERS make the big picture materialize. They are not afraid to use good old-fashioned elbow grease. No task is too menial for them, and they include others in these projects so that new leaders are always in training for future assignments and projects. These leaders work best when allowed freedom to make it happen.

MANAGING LEADERS are great at planning, delegating, organizing, and giving other leaders what they need to complete a task. Attention to detail, evaluation, and processing are strong gifts.

SHEPHERDING LEADERS show love, care, concern, nurture, and understanding in all areas of leadership. When working in a team, constant prayer from these leaders will lift up the entire team.

SPIRITUAL LEADERS focus on the disciplines of prayer, meditation, and discernment. These leaders will keep the team grounded. They are able to bring an entire group back into focus when discussions get muddled or out of sync with the team assignment or God's intent for the church.

Questions to consider when building a team of leaders:

✔ What gifts does this person display that complement the task at hand?

✔ How will this person work with others who have the same or different gifts?

✔ What other roles might we need, and what gifts are needed to fulfill the available leadership position(s)?

Use this inventory to:

■ Identify the leadership style of the people selected to serve.

■ Consider the role they may best serve: coordinator, chairperson, consultant.

How and Where to Find Leaders

Personal invitation is the best way to enlist leadership participation and support. Consider the following ideas for identifying leaders:

- ☐ Check out existing groups in the church.
- ☐ Seek those in professional leadership positions outside the church.
- ☐ Conduct spiritual-gifts inventories for new and/or existing members; maintain a gifts file.
- ☐ Use your gifts file!
- ☐ Informally interview potential candidates by checking their interest level in your project.
- ☐ Identify individuals who are respected by members of the congregation and staff.

- ☐ Identify individuals who are respected by their family and friends.
- ☐ Observe and note who completes tasks.
- ☐ Encourage involvement from people who express dissatisfaction with how things are going, who also offer constructive solutions.
- ☐ Identify those who are proactive rather than reactive in their behaviors.
- ☐ Talk to people about the future and measure their receptiveness and responses. Are they positive?

Questions to ask when selecting leaders:

- ✔ Why or why not are new members considered for leadership positions?
- ✔ When is it not a good time or a valid reason to invite someone to be a leader?
- ✔ What leadership role fits this person's style?

How Do You Develop Leaders? One Step at a Time!

Even individuals who exhibit leadership abilities need nurturing and training to grow stronger and more effective in their roles. Consider the following process to guide potential leaders into leadership positions:

DESIGN (MODELING): As you consider the type of leader you need, begin by modeling leadership skills. Assist people in identifying these skills as they see themselves using them.

STUDY (MENTORING): Looking at all the tasks that need to be completed, allow potential leaders to work along with you. This builds ownership and excitement and a willingness to continue.

PLAN (MONITORING): How's it going? Are all parties involved and working as a team with a common goal in mind? Continue to think as a unit, focused on the task.

ACT (DELEGATING): It's time to let a potential leader work alone.

TEND (MULTIPLYING): As leaders surface and gain skills, let them begin this process and draw in more leaders.

Adapted from "The One-Step Principle for Developing Leaders," Dale Galloway, 9/97 *Net Results*.

Questions to ask when mentoring leaders:

- ✔ Are existing leaders exhibiting the same values that they require of new leaders?
- ✔ How does our congregation recognize and affirm people with the gift of leadership?
- ✔ What intentional leadership development opportunities exist in our congregation?

HEALTH

DESIGN

STUDY

PLAN

ACT

TEND

VISION TEAM BASICS

What is a vision team and how do we establish one? Good question! The governing board of the congregation has the responsibility of assembling a group called the vision team.

Why a Vision Team?

The overall goal of the vision team is to design and oversee the fivefold turnaround process: design, study, plan, act, and tend.

The desired end result of this entire process is "for each member to have a moment of divine insight that breaks into their frozen paradigms of thought and releases them to a new, shared vision for the parish" (*Catching the Next Wave*, p. 38).

Before the congregation becomes involved during the study phase, the team will design or lay out the road map that the process will follow.

Although every step cannot be predetermined, mapping out a plan will reduce anxiety in the team and in the congregation, and will keep everyone focused. How do you begin?

How to Assemble the Vision Team

A team of 6 to 12 members is recommended. Although size may vary by congregation, too small a group may not give sufficient representation and too large a group can become unwieldy.

It is best to begin by assessing the natural constituencies in the congregation, and select leaders from among those groups.

This is a project that requires significant commitment in time and energy. Choose members wisely and only after prayerful consideration.

Utilize the leadership inventories provided in this workbook to select the right leaders for the right positions.

> **REMEMBER** Begin every step of this journey with prayer!
>
> The vision team stays one half step ahead of the congregation to plan. It never works on its own—this is a congregational process. Understand that God has called this team to be shakers and movers. God will reveal the vision for this congregation through the members of this team, the process they design, and congregational members who are partners in the process.

What Does the Vision Team Do?

The job description for the vision team is threefold:

Design a process by which the congregation decides on a vision for the future.

Facilitate the gathering and compilation of the research that the congregation needs to build its vision.

Enhance communication within the congregation about the process.

The vision team completes its task when the congregation is ready to implement its mission strategies. The governing board will be responsible for establishing the subsequent task groups needed to act on the plan. These task groups follow the same process: design, study, plan, act, and tend. The journey continues with more people involved and the congregational mission rejuvenated.

Who Are the Members of the Vision Team?

GOD: Your leader in this quest is God.

PASTOR: The pastor provides spiritual guidance, preaches the word and administers the Sacraments, reinforces the importance of prayer, and shares knowledge of the congregation with the team.

TEAM LEADER: The team leader is a strong lay leader who is respected in the congregation and has skills to convene meetings. Helpful traits include being a visionary, a good listener, an objective thinker, and having the ability to communicate the needs of others clearly.

OTHER LAY LEADERS: Potential members from various groups—choir, Bible study groups, committees, young-adult groups—provide representation of the congregation. Variations in ages, gender, and experiences help to round out the team. Each will take on roles as determined by needs of the team.

OTHER KEY STAFF: If appropriate, include other staff members who can contribute to the process.

SUBGROUPS: At various times during this process, additional task groups may be established to gather data. This involves more people without growing the team too large.

Discussion questions

- What are the natural groupings in our congregation?
- Who are the potential leaders in these groups?
- What would be a good-sized team for our congregation?
- Who exhibits the gifts required for serving on this team?
- Who might be a candidate for the position of team leader?
- What other roles or positions (recorder, communications, etc.) might this team need?
- Who might serve in these positions?
- What other key staff people could contribute to the group?
- What existing groups may serve as task subgroups?

GETTING THE DESIGN PHASE MOVING

When the vision team is in place and ready to work, the first task is to get a handle on the big picture and to lay out a road map for the turn-around process. An understanding of the following concepts is necessary before the vision team begins work on the design phase.

VISION TEAM: Study the following goals and make them an intentional part of the entire process.

Design to build common language and concepts. As the vision team and congregation study the congregation, the community, and the Bible, new concepts and terms will emerge or familiar ones will be understood in new ways. The process needs to integrate methods for the congregation to explore and define these concepts and terms together so that they are widely understood.

Design to strengthen faith. Make individual and corporate prayer, Bible study, and reflection a priority as the congregation seeks a shared vision.

Design for a healthier life together. Plan opportunities for people to interact with each other in the light of Scripture and prayer. This creates healthier attitudes and a healthier means of living together as a faith community.

Keys to a successful design

- Involve a diverse group of members.
- Use thorough and accessible research.
- Create opportunities for people to participate at different levels of involvement.
- Respect the existing church calendar; time activities carefully.
- Don't rush the process.
- Utilize a variety of communication methods.

Moving through the process, use these questions to evaluate how well the team is supporting the goals of the process:

- Have common concepts been identified?
- Are these concepts accepted by the majority?
- Is the language being used free from multiple meanings?
- Is the language being used clear?
- Are participants expressing new thoughts and ideas?
- Are attitudes changing?
- Are members praying with and for each other?
- Is spiritual nurturing happening through Bible studies, prayer, and listening to one another?
- Are conflicts surfacing and being addressed in a constructive manner?
- Are respect and trust growing among participants?

Understanding a Shared Vision

The most effective way to begin to turn around a congregation's negative trends is to establish a God-inspired, **shared vision** for mission. Involving as many people as possible creates ownership and builds a strong foundation upon which to build.

There are five potential outcomes when attempting to establish a shared vision (*Catching the Next Wave: Leadership Strategies for Turn-Around Congregations*, pp. 34–35).

COMMITMENT
Members of the congregation feel true ownership of the vision.

ENROLLMENT
Members are committed to making the vision happen but do not own the vision.

GENUINE COMPLIANCE
Individuals understand the benefits of the vision and will do what is expected of them.

FORMAL COMPLIANCE
Individuals do what the formal systems require of them, but no more.

GRUDGING COMPLIANCE
Individuals do not share the vision but do what they must to maintain their positions of respect within the system.

Organizing for a Shared Vision

☐ Pray!

☐ The goal of the turn-around process is 100 percent genuine commitment, but the reality is that there will be people at all levels of commitment.

☐ Design a process that strives for the largest number of people truly owning the shared vision.

☐ Respect people where they are in this process and encourage them to become more involved.

☐ Complete inventories as a team before using them in large groups.

☐ Anticipate the information the congregational groupings might need in various stages of the turn-around process.

☐ Gather research into easy-to-understand formats. Utilize graphs and charts for comparisons and presentations.

> **REMEMBER** The vision team stays one step ahead of others involved in this process to maintain momentum and focus.

FIRST STEPS TOWARD A SHARED VISION

I f members of the vision team haven't read the book *Catching the Next Wave: Leadership Strategies for Turn-Around Congregations*, do so before moving ahead with the process and team plans. Understanding the big picture helps the team through each phase.

The book lays out a complete plan for a turn-around process. Study the book carefully. Review the inventories in this workbook. Begin to estimate the time and resources you will need to complete each phase. Use a regular calendar to decide meeting dates and times. Maintain a master calendar to assist in ongoing planning. A large, dry-erase type that covers a calendar year might be helpful. A Gantt chart, as illustrated on page 101 of *Catching the Next Wave,* is another way to organize tasks, set up an anticipated schedule, and understand how some activities might overlap others. Using the Gantt chart at this stage also prepares the team for scheduling the implementation of designated mission strategies.

> **REMEMBER** Not every step can be initially scheduled, but anticipating future steps is part of the process. It's time to get started. Go, team!

Steps to Include on a Calendar or Chart

☐ Study mission and vision (use worksheets and book).
- Who are we as a congregation?
- Does our congregation have a mission statement?
- Does our congregation have a vision statement?
- How will we update these documents?
- How will we create these documents?
- How long might this process take?

☐ Develop a statement of the chief complaint (use workbook and book).
- Who will do this?
- What method will we use?
- How long will it take?

☐ If not already done, decide on the health status of the congregation (use workbook and book).
- Is our congregation healthy enough to engage in a turn-around process?
- Is conflict resolution needed?
- Is an outside consultant required?

☐ Study the congregation and community using the inventories, checklists, and methods provided in this workbook to identify outside sources of information and gather data.

- What data do we need?
- What data is available from within our congregation?
- What data is necessary to gather from outside sources?
- Which inventories will be used?
- How long will this process take?

☐ Take time to understand and review the way the different systems within the congregation are reacting to this process.
- Do we allow time between each phase for people to catch up?
- Do we allow time to deal with tension and conflict?
- Do we allow time for evaluations of our progress?
- Do we allow time for people to absorb information? (A new idea is better accepted when it is no longer a new idea!)

☐ Build mission strategies to support the vision. (Use a Gantt chart or a PERT diagram to layout the plan.)
- How will we decide what strategies fit our vision?
- How will we decide what strategies will require additional research and study?

☐ Complete the task as a team and turn over the plan for action to the governing board.

UNDERSTANDING MISSION AND VISION

By the time the vision team gets to the study phase, they will have already studied what mission and vision statements are and what they do. However, the real work on developing these statements begins in the study phase with the congregation participating. Begin with definitions, proceed with study, and move into development of the mission statement. The vision statement is best developed at the end of the study phase when the congregation has learned more about itself and the local community in which it serves. Use the material on the following pages to support the tasks of the study phase.

Before working with the congregation, prepare by studying Chapter 4, "Distinguishing Mission and Vision," from *Catching the Next Wave*, pages 44–54.

Ways to use this information:

- In the vision team study phase
- With the congregation when developing the mission and vision statements
- Enlarged or reproduced as an overhead and/or handout for presentations

HEALTH
DESIGN
STUDY
PLAN
ACT
TEND

Mission

Definition

A mission statement is a broad, general statement of purpose for the body of Christ, the church.

"Mission is the purpose of the entire body of Christ and each part of the body . . . serves that central purpose" (p. 46).

Characteristics of a Mission Statement

BIBLICAL: Built on a solid biblical foundation

PHILOSOPHICAL: Big-picture orientation

INSPIRATIONAL: Excites people

DYNAMIC: Uses action words

MEMORABLE: Easy to recite/memorize

Vision

Definition

A vision statement is specific, detailed, and describes how the congregation lives out its mission now and into the future.

"And yet, each part of the body, whether the hand or the foot, has a very specific service to contribute that is unique to that part of the body. Vision identifies that unique service" (p. 46).

Characteristics of a Vision Statement

GOD-GIVEN: Divine revelation to God's people

STRATEGIC: States how to achieve the big picture

UNIQUE: Customized to each congregation

DYNAMIC: Describes specific actions

CONCISE: Easy to remember but detailed enough to give direction.

FUTURE-ORIENTED: A step in faith!

HEALTH · DESIGN · STUDY · PLAN · ACT · TEND

DEVELOPING A MISSION STATEMENT

Consider these basic steps as you develop or review your mission statement with the congregation.

PRAY. What does God want our congregation to do? Ask for guidance and strength in this process.

STUDY. What is your biblical understanding of mission? Use the Mission Statement worksheets on pages 24–25 or the reflections on pages 76–80.

ASSIMILATE INFORMATION. Translate the biblical understanding of mission into a one- or two-sentence statement that answers these questions:
- ✔ Who are we?
- ✔ What is our purpose?
- ✔ What is God calling us to do?
- ✔ What will we do to answer God's calling?

EVALUATE. Review definition and characteristics of a mission statement. Does this mission statement meet these criteria? If you already have a mission statement review it using the same process and criteria. Make adjustments.

TRY IT ON FOR A WHILE. Live with it, pray about it, and finally, commit to it.

Already have a mission statement?

Evaluate the statement using the definition of mission and the characteristics of a mission statement (p. 21). Does it need revisions? Could it be updated or refreshed? Use whatever portion of this process that applies to your situation. Whether this is a new statement or an existing one, make sure the congregation knows the statement, believes in it, and supports it. The study phase has begun!

How to Introduce the Statement to the Congregation

- ☐ Monthly newsletter
- ☐ Weekly bulletin
- ☐ Announcements during worship
- ☐ Sermons
- ☐ Banners
- ☐ Flyers posted on bulletin board
- ☐ Handouts available in church office and at information booth or kiosk
- ☐ Handouts distributed during Sunday school to be discussed in classes
- ☐ Annual report
- ☐ Bible studies on mission and vision

How to Storyboard

- ☐ Use dry-erase boards or newsprint to record all information from small groups.
- ☐ Identify main categories; print them on clean dry-erase board or on individual self-adhesive notes stuck to a clean wall.
- ☐ Identify phases or words; print them under main categories.
- ☐ Move pieces around until all categories and parts of categories are clearly sorted.
- ☐ Arrange information into phrases, then connect the phrases to create a statement.

(Use this process for group development of a mission statement. See p. 24.)

Sample Meeting Agenda for
Group Development of a Mission Statement

- Welcome

- Share goal of this meeting: To begin developing a congregational mission statement

- Icebreaker: Take the time to get to know each other or relax a crowd that already knows each other.

- Devotions

- Opening prayer

- Vision team report
  - Where are we in our journey?
  - Define *mission* and *vision*.
  - Define meeting process.

- Small groups: Break into small groups for prayer and study with each group using a different worksheet (see p. 25). With more than four groups, duplicate worksheets as needed.

- Reconvene: In the large group, record and assimilate all feedback.
  - Sort and identify those phrases that identify your congregation's understanding of mission.
  - Use the storyboard process to categorize data (see p. 22).
  - Time permitting, draft a statement with the group, or
  - If desired, set another meeting to continue the process with the group, or
  - An initial draft may be assigned to the vision team using the data from this group.
  - Another meeting may be scheduled to review, adapt, and/or adopt the initial draft produced by the vision team.
  - Be sure to evaluate your statement using the definition and criteria for a mission statement.

- Closing remarks: Where do we go from here?
  - Decide if you will live with the statement for a while or introduce the statement to the congregation now.
  - Plan how to introduce the mission statement to the congregation.
  - Discuss other studies to be completed.
  - Discuss other models for future meetings.
  - Identify potential subgroups and interested individuals to assist with other studies in the study phase.

- Closing prayer and adjournment

Extra preparations to consider

- [ ] Have a potluck before the meeting.
- [ ] Open with music.
- [ ] Serve refreshments during a break.
- [ ] Recognize people who have already been working on this process.
- [ ] Have copy(ies) of *Catching the Next Wave: Leadership Strategies for Turn-Around Congregations* available for reference.
- [ ] Supply a printed agenda.
- [ ] Use overheads and/or handouts of mission and vision definitions and characteristics for the presentation.
- [ ] Have paper, pencils, self-adhesive notes, index cards, markers, newsprint, dry erase boards, and Bibles ready.
- [ ] Provide worksheets adapted from samples for small-group study.
- [ ] Before closing with prayer, sing a favorite hymn or have a brief testimony about faith.

Lose your focus?
Participants frustrated?
Stop and PRAY!

MISSION STATEMENT WORKSHEETS

The worksheets on the following page are designed to be used with "Developing a Mission Statement" and "Sample Meeting Agenda" on pages 22–23. However, they can be used in a variety of settings, depending on your congregation's needs, personality, and size.

☐ Utilize adult Sunday morning small groups and other natural groupings of people to complete this process.

☐ Have several large-group meetings.

☐ Have multiple small-group meetings in people's homes.

The Vision Team Preparation

☐ Work through these Bible texts and questions before using them with the congregation.

☐ What other scriptures may be studied to assist in forming a mission statement? Note the Bible studies printed on pages 76–80.

_____

_____

_____

☐ How can you adapt these worksheets or the settings in which they are used to make them work for your congregation?

_____

_____

_____

_____

_____

Worksheet 1: Biblical Study

In your small group, read the following scriptures:
Matthew 28:19–20; Mark 16:15; Luke 9:1–6; Luke 14:23.

Assignment: Use the key questions below for guidance
and reflection as you summarize your interpretation of
what these verses say about mission.
- Who are we?
- What is our purpose?
- What is God calling us to do?
- What will we do to answer God's calling?

Suggestions: Look for key words and/or phrases in the
scripture verses. Look for repeated themes and common
patterns.

Worksheet 2: Biblical Study

In your small group, read the following scriptures:
Matthew 28:19–20; Luke 24:46–47; Acts 26:14–18; John
20:21.

Assignment: Use the key questions below for guidance
and reflection as you summarize your interpretation of
what these verses say about mission.
- Who are we?
- What is our purpose?
- What is God calling us to do?
- What will we do to answer God's calling?

Suggestions: Look for key words and/or phrases in the
scripture. Look for repeated themes and common
patterns.

Worksheet 3: Biblical Study

In your small group, read the following scriptures:
Matthew 28:19–20; Acts 1:8; Romans 10:14–15, 17.

Assignment: Use the key questions below for guidance
and reflection as you summarize your interpretation of
what these verses say about mission.
- Who are we?
- What is our purpose?
- What is God calling us to do?
- What will we do to answer God's calling?

Suggestions Look for key words and/or phrases in the
scripture verses. Look for repeated themes and common
patterns.

Worksheet 4: Biblical Study

In your small group, read the following scriptures:
Matthew 28:19–20; Acts 2:46–47; Romans 16:25–27.

Assignment: Use the key questions below for guidance
and reflection as you summarize your interpretation of
what these verses say about mission.
- Who are we?
- What is our purpose?
- What is God calling us to do?
- What will we do to answer God's calling?

Suggestions: Look for key words and/or phrases in the
scripture. Look for repeated themes and common
patterns.

HEALTH

DESIGN

STUDY

PLAN

ACT

TEND

CONSTRUCTING THE CHIEF COMPLAINT

The next step the vision team takes in the study phase is to draft a statement explaining the "chief complaint." In other words, what is the problem that has caused the negative trend and is the motivation to begin a turn-around process?

Purpose of This Statement

This assessment of the congregation's present status serves as a springboard for the congregation to begin understanding itself. The statement continues to serve as a benchmark throughout the turn-around process and at the end reminds the participants of humble beginnings and progress accomplished.

The questionnaire script (found on pages 28–31) is designed as a telephone interview. Mailing a questionnaire to all members is usually not constructive and, therefore, discouraged. Consider the following:

☐ Adapt the questionnaire to fit your language and congregational specifics.

   ✔ What information is needed?

☐ Select a sampling to interview from all or part of the following: staff, governing board, leaders of committees or other groups, or a random selection from the entire membership.

   ✔ What groups will we select participants from?
   ✔ Who will we call?
   ✔ How many interviews will adequately represent our congregation?

☐ A member of the vision team may conduct the survey or monitor the process. Consider forming a task group and involving people who have a telemarketing and marketing background. Someone who can create data-based charts and graphs may be best suited for compiling the data. The vision team and task group helpers may meet and identify common threads that form the basis of the statement. The vision team is responsible for forming the final product representing the congregation's chief complaint in a concise and understandable statement.

   ✔ Who will review the sample and develop our interview form? The vision team? A task group?
   ✔ Who will make the calls?
   ✔ Who will compile the data?
   ✔ How will we form the statement from the data?

How Will You Use This Statement?

- [ ] Share this statement as a starting point and throughout the process with the groups assisting in the turn around.
- [ ] Communicate this to the congregation in multiple ways: written and verbal.
- [ ] Celebrate when progress is made toward understanding and reversing the causes of the chief complaint.
- [ ] Recognize and celebrate when this statement is no longer needed.
- [ ] Use this statement to indicate your humble beginnings in the process.
- [ ] Eventually point out the progress that has been made since this early and humble beginning.
- [ ] Let go of the statement when it is no longer productive to use it as a starting point or evaluation tool.
- [ ] Pray for God's guidance and blessings on this process.

> **The chief complaint should…**
> - [ ] Reflect the main trends identified from the interview process.
> - [ ] Be no more than two sentences long.
> - [ ] Use plain, easy-to-understand language.

Sample Statements

"Community Church is experiencing a lack of growth in membership due to the lack of friendliness, programs, and ministries to young families."

"Community Church is declining because the worship service is not a meaningful experience. Music, language, and style appeal to only a small number of people."

"Many members of Community Church have moved because the area surrounding the church has a new ethnic make-up."

"The people of Community Church feel isolated from each other due to a lack of fellowship activities. The only meetings that take place are committees where nothing ever seems to get done."

Questionnaire and Interviewer Script

The introductory script used by the caller should reflect your situation. The one printed here was developed by Community Lutheran Church, Las Vegas, Nevada. Adapt comments to your specific situations.

This sample is designed for congregations with plateaued or declining membership.

Before conducting the interviews, ask yourselves:

- ✔ Is our congregation plateaued, declining, or close to death?
- ✔ Will those we survey know there is a crisis?
- ✔ How do we frame questions to show honest intentions?

RESPONDENT RECORD

Respondent's Name: _____

Age: _____   Sex: _____

Zip Code: _____   Phone: _____

CALL RECORD   1. Date: Time:

2. Date: Time:

3. Date: Time:

COMMENTS

_____

_____

_____

QUESTIONNAIRE

INTRODUCTORY SCRIPT

(Adapted from "Appendix B," *Shaping Ministry for Your Community*, Raymond Christensen and James Petersen, Augsburg Fortress, 1993.)

Hi, my name is _____. I am calling members of _____ Church to determine if there is a better way to serve our faith community. You are one of a small number of people randomly selected to participate in this survey so your honest answers are very important. Would you be willing to take 10 to 15 minutes to share your opinions? Any information you provide will be kept anonymous (that is, not associated with your name) and the results will be used to make our congregation more responsive to its members.

QUESTIONS

(*Note: Unless instructed otherwise, surveyor simply records responses in the spaces provided.*)

1. How often do you attend a Sunday worship service? (*Read responses.*)
   ___ 3–4 times a month
   ___ 1–2 times a month
   ___ On holidays or special occasions
   ___ Other: _____
   ___ Don't attend because _____ (*Skip to Question 22.*)

2. Which Sunday worship services have you attended? (*Read responses and check all services attended.*) Which do you attend the most often? (*Circle one response.*)
___ 7:30 A.M.
___ 8:30 A.M.
___ 9:45 A.M.
___ 11:00 A.M.
___ 7:00 P.M.

3. Why do you attend this particular service most often? (*Do not read responses. Check all mentioned.*)
___ Time is convenient
___ Like style of service
___ Child care, Sunday school available
___ Friends, family attend this service
___ Other _____

4. Briefly, how would you describe this service if you were telling a friend about it? _____

5. _____ Church offers both traditional and contemporary services. Which do you prefer?
___ Traditional
___ Contemporary

6. Would you prefer to attend a worship service on a weeknight, rather than on Sunday?
___ No
___ Yes, on _____ night.

7. Do you usually come to church . . . ? (*Read responses.*)
___ By yourself   ___ With your spouse
___ With family   ___ With friends
___ Other _____

8. How long have you been a member of _____ Church?
___ Less than 1 year   ___ 11–15 years
___ 1–2 years   ___ 15–20 years
___ 3–5 years   ___ More than 20 years
___ 6–10 years

9. Did you belong to another church before joining _____Church?
___ No   ___ Yes (*Ask, "What denomination?"*)
        ___ Catholic   ___ Lutheran
        ___ Methodist   ___ Baptist
        ___ Presbyterian   ___ Other

10. What would you say is the most important reason you joined this church?_____

11. How important were the following factors in your decision to become a member of _____ Church—very important, somewhat important, or not important?

VI   SI   NI   Location of the church
VI   SI   NI   Times of service
VI   SI   NI   The pastor
VI   SI   NI   Quality of sermons
VI   SI   NI   The fact that it is Lutheran church
VI   SI   NI   Style of worship service
VI   SI   NI   Type of music/hymns used
VI   SI   NI   Size of congregation
VI   SI   NI   Sunday school program
VI   SI   NI   Friends, family are members
VI   SI   NI   Church-related activities

12. Were there any other reasons you decided to join _____ Church?
___ No   ___ Yes. Also because _____

13. How satisfied, on a scale of 1 to 10 (1 = very dissatisfied), are you with the following activities provided by _____ Church? (*Circle DK if respondent says, "Don't know" or "No opinion."*)

1 2 3 4 5 6 7 8 9 10 DK   Ministers/pastors
1 2 3 4 5 6 7 8 9 10 DK   Coffee/fellowship time between services
1 2 3 4 5 6 7 8 9 10 DK   Sunday school
1 2 3 4 5 6 7 8 9 10 DK   Nursery/child care
1 2 3 4 5 6 7 8 9 10 DK   Style of worship service
1 2 3 4 5 6 7 8 9 10 DK   Type of hymns sung
1 2 3 4 5 6 7 8 9 10 DK   Use of drama in the service
1 2 3 4 5 6 7 8 9 10 DK   Degree of informality
1 2 3 4 5 6 7 8 9 10 DK   Size of congregation
1 2 3 4 5 6 7 8 9 10 DK   Ushers at service
1 2 3 4 5 6 7 8 9 10 DK   Variety of church-sponsored activities for youth
1 2 3 4 5 6 7 8 9 10 DK   Variety of church-sponsored activities for families
1 2 3 4 5 6 7 8 9 10 DK   Variety of church-sponsored activities for singles

14. For any of the above items marked 1, 2, 3, or 4, what could be done to improve them? (*Read topics again.*)
_____

15. In which church-related activities have you participated during the past year, and would you participate in this activity again?
    Activity:_____ Y N
    Activity:_____ Y N
    Activity:_____ Y N

16. What other types of activities would you like to see offered?
    _____

17. Overall, how personally involved in your faith would you say you are at this time in your life? (*Read choices.*)
    ___ Very involved
    ___ Somewhat involved
    ___ Uninvolved

18. What do you think _____ Church could do to help members become more involved with their faith and the congregation? _____
    _____

19. Do you have children living at home?
    ___ No
    ___ Yes (*Ask, "What are their ages?"*)
        ___ Younger than 3 years old (*Go to 19a.*)
        ___ 3 to 12 years old (*Skip to 19b.*)
        ___ 13 to 18 years old
        ___ Older than 18

19a. (*If children are less than 3 years old, ask:*) Do you use the nursery for your child while you attend worship?
    ___ No
        I. Why not?_____
        II. When the new expansion program is finished, the nursery will be located right next to the worship area. Will this increase the probability of your using it for your child?
            ___ Yes   ___ No
            ___ Maybe   ___ Don't know
    ___ Yes
        I. How satisfied are you with the care your child receives in the nursery? (*Read responses.*)
            ___ Very satisfied
            ___ Somewhat satisfied
            ___ Somewhat dissatisfied, because
            _____
        II. What suggestions do you have for improving the nursery and its services?

19b. (*If children are between 3 and 12 years old, ask:*)
    I. Do your children attend Sunday school at _____ Church?
        ___ No, because _____
        ___ Yes, the _____ service.

    II. Recently the Sunday school program started using videos along with traditional Sunday school materials to teach Bible lessons in grades 1 through 6. Do you think this is a good idea?
        ___ Yes
        ___ No
        Why or why not? _____

    III. Do your children attend the worship service with you?
        ___ Yes
        ___ No

20. Do you agree, are you neutral, or do you disagree with the following statements:

    A N D   I like the use of banners, signs, and visual materials during the worship service.

    A N D   I enjoy a worship service more when the whole service has one central theme.

    A N D   I like the traditional hymns better than the modern ones.

    A N D   I think the pastors should wear robes.

    A N D   Holy Communion should be offered every Sunday.

    A N D   I enjoy worshiping with formal liturgy.

    A N D   _____ Church does a good job of making people feel welcome.

    A N D   I am glad I'm a member of _____ Church.

    A N D   _____ Church focuses too much on performance and not enough on people.

    A N D   The church needs to focus more on lessons from the Bible and less on practical living issues.

    A N D   _____ Church should be actively involved in community projects such as the soup kitchen.

21. About how many times a year do you invite friends or relatives to visit _____ Church?

22. If you had one, and only one, idea to make the church better, what would it be? _____
_____

(*The next several questions are meant to get an idea of what _____ Church members are like demographically and how they feel about certain topics.*)

23. How concerned would you say you are with the following factors—very concerned, somewhat concerned, or not concerned?

VC SC NC   Finding/keeping affordable housing

VC SC NC   Finding/keeping your job

VC SC NC   Finding/keeping quality child care

VC SC NC   Dealing with stress

VC SC NC   Maintaining personal health/safety

VC SC NC   Finding/providing care for an aging parent

VC SC NC   Providing for the homeless

VC SC NC   Dealing with drug/alcohol abuse

VC SC NC   Dealing with gangs

VC SC NC   Dealing with child abuse

VC SC NC   Dealing with racial/ethnic prejudice

VC SC NC   Developing parenting skills

VC SC NC   Finding direction in life

VC SC NC   Finding spiritual fulfillment

24. How do you enjoy spending your spare time? (*Check all mentioned.*)

___ Athletics/sports   ___ Reading
___ Watching TV   ___ Gambling
___ Crafts   ___ Gardening/yard work
___ Other _____

25. How many people live in your household? _____

26. What is your marital status? (*Read responses.*)
___ Married
___ Divorced
___ Single
___ Widowed

27. What is the highest level of education you have completed? (*Read responses.*)
___ Elementary school
___ Junior high school
___ Some high school
___ High school graduate
___ Some college
___ Trade school
___ Associate degree
___ Bachelors degree
___ Some graduate studies
___ Graduate degree

28. What is your racial/ethnic background? (*Read responses.*)
___ Caucasian
___ Black
___ Asian
___ Hispanic
___ Native American
___ Other _____

29. In which category does your annual total household income fall? (*Read responses.*)
___ Less than $20,000
___ $20,000–$39,999
___ $40,000–$59,000
___ $60,000 or more

CLOSING-COMMENT SCRIPT

Thank you for your time. We greatly appreciate your contribution. Your participation will enable our leadership to develop ministries that are more responsive to our members, guests, and visitors.

READINESS TOOL: CASTING A VISION

All living organisms experience a predictable life cycle. It is a biological fact that the various stages of life include death. If we consider the church a living organism, then this means that some congregations will naturally die. "The death of a congregation is no more a threat to the Christian church than the death of an individual threatens the human race" (*Catching the Next Wave*, p. 12). However, when we compare the congregation to the life cycles and habits of people, we discover that there are ways to prolong life.

It is a scientific fact that people are living longer today. Does this information help the church? Gary McIntosh, professor and church consultant, shares the following information when comparing people to congregations.

PEOPLE WHO LIVE LONGER:	INSIGHTS FOR CONGREGATIONS:
Keep learning and trying new experiences.	Read, attend seminars, try new models for ministry.
Work hard and enjoy it!	The pastor, staff, and people are willing to work hard . . . and have fun!
Organize well.	Plan with organizational guidelines to empower people's goals.
Help others.	Focus on people, make disciples.
Live out passions.	Live a clearly defined vision.
Live resiliently.	Face problems, learn from mistakes.
Stay focused on God.	Pray for growth, expect God to answer prayer.

Adapted from "How To Live To Be 100," Gary McIntosh, *Net Results*, 5/98.

Vision Team Notes

The activities on pages 33–35 may be used at various times with various groups. Use only the activities appropriate for the stage you are in.

The vision team completes all activities before the congregation uses them. The team completes the activities:

☐ When determining the health of the congregation
☐ Before constructing the chief complaint

Then the team uses the activities as a congregational group activity:

☐ Before creating a mission statement
☐ Before creating a shared vision

Activity 1

Present information from the introduction of this workbook and ask for general reactions and comments.

For example:

☐ Introduce "church mapping" and the need to be responsive to a rapidly changing world.

☐ Introduce and describe the phases of the turn-around process and the definition of congregation health.

☐ Describe what is required for a congregational turn around: being open to God's vision and guidance, commitment to work through conflict for the sake of the community and God's purposes.

> ## The church has a choice:
> to die as a result of its resistance to change, or to die in order to live.
>
> —Mike Regele,
> *Death of the Church*

Activity 2

Where is your congregation in its cycle of life? Gather membership or worship attendance statistics for each year of the congregation's life. Plot them on the chart below, then mark where the congregation experienced growth, maturity, and decline.

Discussion questions

✔ Where is our congregation in its life cycle?
✔ Why might our congregation differ from the normal cycle?

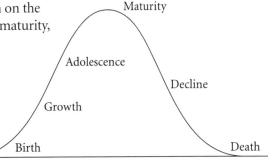

LIFE CYCLE OF A CONGREGATION

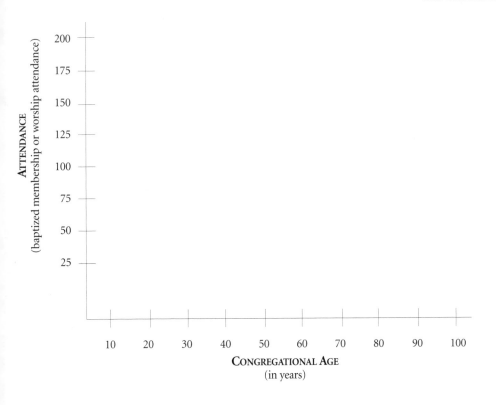

Activity 3

Read background information on pages 11–13 in *Catching the Next Wave: Leadership Strategies for Turn-Around Congregations.*

Discussion questions
- ✔ How might the insights for congregations previously discussed provide opportunities for new growth as illustrated in the diagram?
- ✔ When does the diagram illustrate new efforts for health and growth take place? Why is this important?

Activity 4

Read through these descriptions of congregations and discuss the questions that follow on the next page. Background information for this section is found on pages 20–30 of *Catching the Next Wave: Leadership Strategies for Turn-Around Congregations.*

Name	Description	Readiness to Create a Vision
MISSION START	A young congregation that is intentionally planted by a denomination or by an established congregation	Relatively easy to establish a shared vision for ministry since all members are excited and most likely have fresh attitudes and open minds
RESTART	An older congregation that once had a viable ministry but has declined to the point of death and has had to be restarted again almost as if it were a new mission start-up	More difficult to establish a shared vision for ministry than a mission start congregation, but still manageable due to a decrease in numbers of members and desire to avoid congregational death
MATURE AND DECLINING (PLATEAUED)	A congregation, approximately 35 or more years old, that still maintains some health but is experiencing insignificant growth and little passion for mission	Difficult to change due to established patterns, traditions, attitudes, larger memberships, and common ignorance of problem(s)
TURN-AROUND CONGREGATION	A congregation that has reversed an unhealthy trend of more than five years in one or more of the seven criteria for health: organization, growth, movement, transformation, sensitivity, adaptation, and reproduction; basically healthy but experiencing a negative trend	Are able to work through problems and create a new, shared vision for ministry in the congregation and reverse the negative trend

Discussion questions
- Which category might fit our congregation today? Tomorrow? Why?
- How have other congregations we know lived through these stages?
- What have we learned about our congregation from this exercise?
- Is there conflict in our congregation to address before we continue with the process?
- What can we do to prepare our congregation for the next step in the turn-around process?

Activity 5

Present the following statement and discuss.

"The church has a choice: to die as a result of its resistance to change or die in order to live." Mike Regele, founder of Percept Group (*Death of the Church*, Zondervan Publishing House, 1996).

Discussion questions
- What does this statement mean to us?
- What different ways may a congregation "die in order to live"?
- What might this mean for our congregation?

Summary discussion question
- How is our congregation ready to cast a vision for ministry?

_____
_____
_____
_____
_____
_____
_____
_____
_____

For additional background information, see *Catching the Next Wave: Leadership Strategies for Turn-Around Congregations*, chapters 1–2.

STUDY PHASE TOOLS

The study phase is an intense time of gathering, compiling, evaluating, and summarizing information for and about your congregation. Be thorough, allow time to work and to process, and include as many people as possible in the many different steps.

Vision Team: When the data reveals unresolved conflict, remember to stop the process and deal with the issues. Individuals in your congregation such as social workers and counselors may have the gifts needed to address basic disagreements and conflict. Resources are provided in this workbook, for example, "Managing Conflict in a Turn-Around Congregation" on page 72. If the situation is beyond your ability to handle, seek outside help. See resource list in on page 10 of this workbook.

> **TIP!** Keep all material you gather in a notebook for constant reference, review, and evaluation at any point in time.

Checklist for the Study Phase

☐ Pray!

☐ Study mission and vision by using the Bible studies in this workbook (pp. 76–80) and by reviewing Chapter 4 in *Catching the Next Wave*.

☐ Develop/update a mission statement.

☐ Develop a statement of the chief complaint, identifying the main problem.

☐ Develop a history of present problems to explain, clarify, and support the chief complaint. Utilize questions on pages 57–58 of *Catching the Next Wave* for discussion. Also use the data from the "Is Our Congregation Healthy?" and "Can This Congregation Turn Around?" inventories (pp. 6–10).

☐ Gather congregational history and internal statistics:
- Membership
- Attendance patterns
- Sunday school statistics
- Age and gender demographics
- Giving trends
- Budget growth
- Professional staff, past and present
- Timeline of congregation's key events
- Identification of significant conflicts and how/if they were resolved
- Previous mission/vision statements
- Information from completed inventories

☐ Gather external statistics:
- Local socioeconomic groupings
- Demographics by race, ethnic mix, gender, age, culture, education
- Denominational demographic studies

☐ Discover the congregation's culture and social history (see *Catching the Next Wave*, pp. 60–63). Include:
- Visible congregational structures and groupings
- Long-standing traditions and to whom they belong
- Conscious values openly agreed upon
- Basic assumptions understood but never discussed
- Members' recountings of the congregation's history, their dreams for the future, and their thoughts on what they would like to tell new members
- Data from "Is Our Congregation Healthy?" inventory
- Data gathered from "Can This Congregation Turn Around?" inventory

☐ Consider outside consultants for conflict management.

☐ Assemble a general description of the congregation with information from the various studies. The description should have the following characteristics (see *Catching the Next Wave*, pp. 67–68 for a sample):
- One page in length
- Clarifies what everyone assumes is obvious
- Serves as an identity statement from which to move into the plan stage

> For surely I know the plans I have for you, says the Lord, plans for your welfare and not for your harm, to give you a future with hope.
>
> *Jeremiah 29:11*

Research Materials

☐ Inventories in this workbook

☐ *Counting Your Community: Using Census Statistics as Part of Congregational Planning*, Division for Congregational Ministries, ELCA

☐ *Complete Ministry Audit*, Bill Easum, Abingdon Press, 1996

☐ *Reaching the Unchurched—Creating the Vision, Planning to Grow*, Walt Kallestad and Tim Wright, Augsburg Fortress, 1994

☐ U.S. Bureau of the Census on the Internet at http://www.census.gov

☐ Local library and Chamber of Commerce

☐ Local school board for local school feeder patterns (to determine its effect on your congregation)

☐ Some denominational offices provide community demographics for member congregations. For example, the Evangelical Lutheran Church in America will prepare zip code level census reports for ELCA congregations. (800) NET-ELCA or http://www.elca.org

Suggested Research Models

Methods to gather your data:

☐ Questionnaires to congregational leaders, visitors, or neighbors (written or conducted via the telephone)

☐ Personal interviews

☐ Large-group meetings for members (break into small discussion groups)

☐ Multiple small-group meetings for members

☐ Meetings with existing congregation groupings

☐ Interviews with local businesses to learn what they know about your church

☐ Interviews with leaders of local Christian churches to determine their vision and style of ministry in the community

How to Live with and in the Turn-Around Process

SYSTEMS THINKING is "seeing interrelationships rather than linear cause-effect chains, and seeing processes of change rather than snapshots" (Peter Senge, *The Fifth Discipline*, Currency Doubleday, p. 73).

CHECKLIST FOR HEALTHY CONGREGATIONAL SYSTEMS THINKING

☐ Recognize that people, group, and task relationships overlap and are not linear cause-and-effect chains.

☐ No part of the system is isolated from another.

☐ Evaluate a process of change, not a single action or event.

☐ A change made in one part creates change in another part or even the whole system.

☐ Remember: Matters are never as simple as they appear. Look deeper. Ask "who, what, where, when, why?"

☐ For every action, there is an equal and opposed reaction (Sir Isaac Newton's third law of motion).

☐ Working harder at change without recognizing and dealing with new tensions only spins wheels in the system that, in turn, create more tension.

☐ Stop, think, and process through new challenges, tensions, and conflicts before continuing with a ministry strategy.

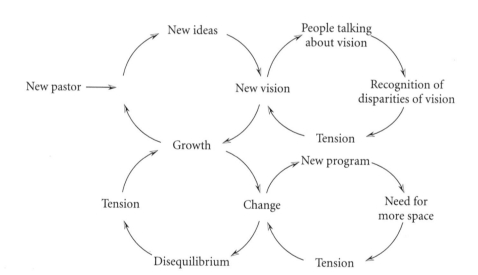

Discussion questions

↳ How have we seen change affecting our congregational system thus far?

↳ What are we learning about our congregational system that we can integrate into our planning?

↳ What issues have surfaced that need to be addressed before we move forward?

Dealing with Change in Any Phase

As the vision team moves through the study phase involving different groups of people, the realization that change is coming will begin to grow. Since most changes are perceived as stepping out of comfort zones, the team needs to be ready to assist people with feelings of insecurity, uncertainty, and loss of confidence. Try these steps:

☐ **Pray**
In our haste of getting the job done, we may forget to include God. Pray throughout this entire process for God's guidance, strength, and blessings.

☐ **Communicate, communicate, communicate**
It takes time for a concept to filter through the entire congregation. Even when an idea can be repeated, do not assume understanding. Use all forms of communication available: announcements during worship, weekly bulletins, monthly newsletters, reviews and updates of the process at the beginning of every meeting, and individual contact/conversation.

☐ **Maintain a positive attitude**
It is essential for leaders to model enthusiasm. Leaders who see the glass half full, instead of half empty, create a positive momentum for the process.

☐ **Maintain visibility**
The vision team is important in the turn-around process. The congregation needs to build a high level of trust during the ongoing relationship between the team and other task groups. Maintain an image of openness and cooperation by being available and willing to discuss questions and concerns.

☐ **Affirm existing and past ministries**
Present the past in a positive manner. Recognize the ministries that are functioning today. Allow perceived failures to become opportunities to learn and grow into the future.

☐ **Involve key leaders**
People who are included in a process are more likely to become advocates. Advocates who are leaders will influence and encourage others.

☐ **Expect conflict**
Change naturally creates challenge, tension, and conflict. Identify the conflict, address it, and channel the energy generated into positive actions. Remember systems thinking!

☐ **Don't move too quickly**
In the study phase, people may become excited or impatient and want to move ahead. Explain the need to gather and study all the data available before moving to the plan or act stage.

☐ **Don't wait forever to move to the next step**
It is possible to get stuck; this will kill momentum! Evaluate. Decide how long to spend in one area of study or when you have sufficient data to move to the plan phase.

Vision Team Attitude Check

The study phase is an intense time. The team is spending time and energy on gathering the data. There will be tensions and conflicts to face and resolve. How can you keep your focus healthy, positive, and in tune with God?

It's time for an attitude check! Answer these questions as individual team members. Circle the number that applies to your current feelings about your participation on the team.

Prayer and devotions are part of my everyday life.

I could be better at this.   I do this well.

1   2   3   4   5

Biblical reflection and prayer are a part of every team meeting.

We could be better at this.   We do this well.

1   2   3   4   5

I delegate tasks to involve more people.

We could be better at this.   We do this well.

1   2   3   4   5

I am willing to take risks for the sake of the church's mission.

I could be better at this.   I do this well.

1   2   3   4   5

I project courage in taking risks.

I could be better at this.   I do this well.

1   2   3   4   5

I enthusiastically accept new assignments.

I could be better at this.   I do this well.

1   2   3   4   5

I am compassionate when others express concerns.

I could be better at this.   I do this well.

1   2   3   4   5

I am willing to discuss my concerns with the team.

I could be better at this.   I do this well.

1   2   3   4   5

I update team members on all information I accumulate.

I could be better at this.   I do this well.

1   2   3   4   5

I participate on this team to serve God, not my own needs.

I could be better at this.   I do this well.

1   2   3   4   5

ARE WE A DISCIPLING CONGREGATION?

How prevalent are the following questions in your congregation? "Why are all the same people doing the work of the church?" "Where are all the newer members?" "Why don't more visitors come back?"

The following assessments help to answer these questions. The vision team completes these inventories first and prepares in advance any material that may be necessary for discussions when used with congregational groups for study. The assessments do not have to be repeated with the congregation but can provide the data the vision team presents to the congregation for discussion and assessment. For additional inventories on this subject, order *The Discipling Congregation: Strengthening Your Congregation's Incorporation Ministry* by David Poling-Goldenne (ELCA, 1995), (800) 328-4648.

Assessment Tool A
A Basic Study of Existing Membership Integration and Discipleship Activity

Task 1: Define *membership* in your congregation.

Task 2: Define *membership integration* in your congregation.

Task 3: Define a *discipling congregation*.

Task 4: List the people who have joined your congregation over the past year.

> **Questions to answer:**
> - What are their current levels of participation?
> - How often do they worship?
> - Do new members complete a spiritual-gifts assessment?
> - In what ways have they been invited to use their gifts and skills in our congregation or community?
> - Are they involved in a small group or attending a class?
> - Have they made new friends?
> - What percentage of new members are effectively plugged into leadership roles (choir, teachers, ushers, worship assistants, etc.)?
> - How many people participate in activities/programs but do not formally join? What might be the reasons for this?
> - What strategies are in place to serve longtime visitors/ guests?

Helpful tips

- ☐ Understand the goal: Listen with an ear to how you might strengthen your congregation's ministry.
- ☐ Form groups of no more than eight people.
- ☐ Appoint one person to convene each group.
- ☐ Appoint one person to record responses in each group.
- ☐ The rest of the vision team or task group may sit silently outside the circle and listen. (This should not be an overwhelming number of people.)
- ☐ Encourage people to be honest.
- ☐ Do not ask questions in an accusatory way.
- ☐ Use open-ended questions.
- ☐ Avoid being defensive.
- ☐ Include time for introduction, refreshments, and fellowship.
- ☐ Open and close with prayer.
- ☐ Provide a biblical reflection (Romans 12, 1 Corinthians 12).
- ☐ Consider individual interviews as an alternative.

Task 5: List people who have become less active or inactive in the last three years. Do not count people who have moved.

Questions to answer:
- How many people did we list?
- How does this number compare to the number of new members received during the same period of time?
- How many people were connected to a ministry that was discontinued and did not connect to another ministry?
- Is there anyone (staff or team) assigned to follow up on membership activity levels?

Task 6: Study the worship patterns of your congregation.

Questions to answer:
- What percentage of our members worship in any given week?
- What percentage of members worship once a month or less?
- On the average, how many new people visit our worship services during the course of one year?
- What percentage of visitors/guests actually become members?
- What percentage of members attend worship without formally joining the congregation?

Adapted from *The Disciplining Congregation*, David Poling-Goldenne, ELCA, 1995.

Summary reflection questions
- What does the data from this survey suggest about our congregation's ability to disciple, incorporate, and retain members?
- What strengths and weaknesses can we discover from this data?
- What seems to be working well that our congregation can build on?
- Does our congregational leadership define membership differently than newer members define it? What new developments in this area do you see?
- Are the present definitions of membership, membership integration, and discipleship in need of revision?

List three implications for further conversation. How might you use this information? Compile data from this assessment into report form for reflection, evaluation, and future reference.

Assessment Tool B
Relationship Ratios

Another way to assess your congregation's strengths in discipling is by using ratios established by church growth studies. Effective discipling congregations need to have their ratios in order. Evaluate your congregation using the following ratios that come from the Win Arn Growth Report.

> TIP! Establish a current, accurate active membership number with which to make ratio comparisons. Use your average worship attendance if no other figure is available or possible to determine.

ROLE TASK RATIO (60:100)

There should be at least 60 roles and tasks available for every 100 members in your congregation.

A role or a task refers to a specific position, function, or responsibility in the congregation (choir, committee, team members). Any fewer than 60 roles/tasks/ministries per 100 members creates an environment that produces inactive members.

- ☐ List all activities in your congregation in each of the following areas of ministry: worship, nurture, witness, and service.
- ☐ How do the number of tasks or roles compare to your active membership number?

GROUP RATIO (7:100)

There should be at least seven groups in your congregation for every 100 members.

The consequence of too few groups for members to build meaningful relationships is a high rate of inactives exiting.

Creating an effective group life is a fundamental building block upon which incorporation and retention depend.

- ☐ Identify all small groups, classes, or fellowship opportunities now present in your congregation.
- ☐ How does this figure compare to your membership number?

NEW GROUPS RATIO (1:5)

Of the groups that now exist in your congregation, one of every five (20%) should have been started in the past two years.

Groups tend to reach a "saturation" point somewhere between 9 and 18 months following their formation. The remedy is to add new groups. New groups bring new growth and new people.

- ☐ List all new groups established within the last two years.
- ☐ Which are still active? Why?
- ☐ When some stopped meeting, were other groups established? Were people integrated into other groups?
- ☐ Are new groups intentionally created and open to new people?
- ☐ How does your number compare in the stated ratio?

FRIENDSHIP RATIO (1:7)

Each new member should be able to identify at least seven friends in your congregation within the first six months.

The first six months are critical. If they have not made friends by then, they are likely to be on their way out the back door.

- ☐ How many new members have established at least seven friends within the first six months of membership?
- ☐ How can you learn this information?
- ☐ How does this compare to the ratio stated?

From *The Disciplining Congregation: Strengthening Your Congregation's Incorporation Ministry,* David Poling-Goldenne, ELCA, 1995.

Catching the Next Wave: Leadership Strategies for Turn-Around Congregations. Copyright © Augsburg Fortress. May be reproduced for local use.

COMMITTEE/TEAM RATIO (1:5)

One of every five committee/team members should have joined your congregation within the last two years.

Regularly review the committee/team structure in your congregation to ensure this ratio. Doing so will encourage an openness in the power structure and assure that your church remembers its real mission.

☐ List all committees/teams and determine how many people have joined these groups within the last five years.

☐ How does this number compare to the stated ratio?

VISITOR RATIO (3:10)

Of the first-time visitors who live in your congregation's ministry areas, three of every ten should be actively involved within one year.

Some studies indicate that with an effective strategy, congregations can see four of every ten visitors return a second time.

An incorporation strategy that focuses on second-time visitors can result in 70 percent to 75 percent joining within a year. In contrast, nongrowing congregations typically see only 5 percent to 12 percent of their first-time visitors actually join.

☐ How do you keep track of visitor/guest attendance?

☐ How do you get this information now?

☐ How are you intentional about incorporating visitors?

☐ How does your number compare with the stated ratio?

STAFF RATIO (1:150)

Your congregation should have one full-time staff member for every 150 persons in worship.

If the ratio reaches 1:225 to 1:250, it is unusual to see any significant increase in active membership. While more persons may join the congregation, the back door will open wider and more people will leave.

☐ How does the number of staff compare to the stated ratio?

☐ Are you over- or understaffed?

☐ Why might the number of staff needed in your congregation not match this ratio?

☐ How do you compare to the ratio stated for size of staff?

Adapted from *The Disciplining Congregation*, David Poling-Goldenne, ELCA, 1995.

Final Summary and Evaluation Tasks

☐ Review your initial definitions of membership, membership integration, and discipleship. How have they changed after these assessments?

☐ Make a list of those things that have surfaced as strengths in your congregation. What do you do well? What is working? What seems to be effective in involving and incorporating people?

☐ Make a list of those things that have surfaced as weaknesses in your congregation. What is lacking? What is not working?

☐ Compile this data into effective forms for reading and presentation.

VISION TEAM: Is any additional research needed before using these assessments with other groups?

FROM MAINTENANCE TO MISSION
Assessment Tool A
Determining Potential for Mission Focus

In 1993 Aid Association for Lutherans, a fraternal insurance agency, engaged in a series of research studies called the Church Membership Initiative (CMI). The research was designed to discover factors that contribute to congregational growth and decline in Lutheran congregations. The following traits were found to be present in most growing, mission-driven congregations:

- They saw themselves in mission beyond the current membership.

- The lay and clergy leadership had a shared vision.

- Multiple entry points were intentionally provided by the congregation for easy access into the life of the congregation.

- They were flexible in methods communicating an unchanging message within a changing world. They used multiple styles of communication to reach a wide variety of people interests.

- They were action oriented. They were not willing to be limited by challenges of size, language, resources, or conflict.

- They adopted localized, contextualized answers to questions about how they could achieve their mission. They adapted programs to fit their needs and neighborhood.

VISION TEAM: Study these character traits of growing congregations, then evaluate your congregation using these characteristics.

☐ What information may you wish to gather before using this assessment with the congregation?

☐ Define maintenance focus and mission focus.

☐ Prepare overheads or handouts when using with congregational groups in the study phase. Use this presentation to introduce the next assessment tool.

Assessment Tool B:
Why Do Congregations Need to Become "Mission Driven"?

(Adapted from *The Reaching Congregation—Tips and Tools to Strengthen Intentional Outreach*, David Poling-Goldenne, et al, ELCA, 1996, p. 3.)

A LOOK AT TWO CONGREGATIONS

Trinity Church is a congregation experiencing change. This church once claimed an important place in the community. Today Trinity struggles to discover its mission. Years ago its tall spire lit up at night, reminding many of Matthew's words, "You are the light of the world. A city set on a hill cannot be hid." People driving by the church or meeting in the local cafe knew about Trinity. For years, Trinity could trace a legacy of strong preaching, an active youth group, and a heart for world missions. Today, they are struggling to keep the lights lit on the spire. A majority of Trinity people still remember the good ol' days when Sunday school classes were filled and youth and adults together attended the youth group. But things have changed. Some blame it on the changing community. Others look around and point to the aging members. Although they have been debt-free for almost a generation, their annual giving totals less than $50,000 with an average Sunday attendance of less than 50 people. In recent months, they have been engaged in a study of their purpose for ministry. What is their mission? One bright spot remains—their savings account. With over $500,000 in the bank, they have some options. Where is God calling them?

First Lutheran Church, another congregation, has a similar legacy. Their charter quotes the Lutheran foundation, "since all have sinned and fall short of the glory of God, they are justified by God's grace as a gift, through the redemption which is in Christ Jesus" (Romans 3:23-24). Today, First Lutheran does not look like the congregation it did a decade ago. At the point of closing its doors, First embraced the last hope—-a new mission to their neighborhood. It was not easy to change. It was painful to see some of the traditions left in the past. But most would agree: "Change was worth it!" Today it has an active Sunday school and two vibrant worship services on Sunday. One is traditional while the other is in an alternate style. In the last ten years, they have planted a mission congregation and have become a beacon of light in their own community. People of all backgrounds are rolling up their sleeves and sharing their excitement over First's mission. They have discovered joy in God's calling.

These two congregations, like many congregations, are on the edge of change. In many corners of the church, leaders are saying, "This is not the world we were trained to serve in." Mainline congregations are no longer a collection of European immigrants unified by common ancestry and a common hymnal. A generation ago, mission meant reaching out overseas. Today, the largest mission field is in our neighborhoods. And these neighborhoods are more diverse, with decreasing religious background and less knowledge of Christian traditions.

VISION TEAM: Compile responses for use in the plan phase. Compare vision team ideas to those of the congregational groups. Did more information surface? Is data similar or different? What would account for differences?

Discussion questions
- What similarities exist between these two congregations and our congregation?
- How is life in our congregation different today than 10 years ago? Five years ago?
- How do we engage in mission in an increasingly "foreign" neighborhood?
- What assets are we sitting on that could be put to more active use?

Assessment Tool C:
"Eight Critical Shifts" Worksheet

(From The Reaching Congregation—Tips and Tools to Strengthen Intentional Outreach, David Poling-Goldenne, et al, ELCA, 1996, p. 3.)

Reflect on the following characteristics exhibited by most effective mission-oriented congregations. Determine where you feel your congregation might fall on the scale (1 = focused on maintenance, 10 = fully engaged in mission). Share your thoughts with the whole group when all have completed the worksheet.

> **VISION TEAM:** Complete the worksheet first. Verify and clarify all language for use in congregation groups in the study phase. Define mission and vision for the congregation groups before having them complete the assessment.

1. Clear Vision

We live in a complex world with "information overload." People yearn for a clear vision of their personal destiny in God's plan for history. Articulate the vision and communicate what is expected to pursue it. People will be motivated into action knowing the values and beliefs of your congregation.

FROM MAINTENANCE MINISTRY:
- Identity by heritage
- Emphasis on information

- Mission based on obligation
- Institutional vision from above
- Abstract, vague, distant

TO EFFECTIVE MISSION
- Identity by beliefs and values
- Emphasis on motivation and faith sharing
- Mission based on love
- Team vision from below

- Specific, clear, and heart-felt

Rate your progress: 1   2   3   4   5   6   7   8   9   10

2. Intentional Planning

Intentionally plan for mission using action strategies to transform lives. Provide easy access for newcomers and deepening spirituality for adult participants. Strategize hands-on ministries to your neighborhood and congregational ownership for world mission. Unite faith sharing and social service. According to the ELCA Department of Research and Evaluation 1996 report, ELCA congregations that neglected to plan experienced a 17 percent loss in average worship attendance.

FROM MAINTENANCE MINISTRY:
- Consensus before action
- Redundant planning
- Committees
- Administration
- Comfort within the membership

TO EFFECTIVE MISSION
- Streamlined decision making
- Do it . . . and learn
- Spirituality and mission teams
- Ministry
- Mission beyond the membership

Rate your progress: 1   2   3   4   5   6   7   8   9   10

3. Flexible Support Systems

Responding to emerging needs requires flexibility and a willingness to adapt infrastructure to fit mission priorities. Move toward organizational structures that are more fluid and streamlined. Encourage new ministries. Embrace the attitude that nothing is impossible in Christ!

FROM MAINTENANCE MINISTRY:
- Rigid, "concrete-like" bureaucracy
- Hierarchical flowchart
- "We've always done it that way."
- Ministry limited by budget
- Limited family-focused ministries

TO EFFECTIVE MISSION
- Flexible, "clay-like" support systems
- Web-like, relational flowchart
- "Let's try it this way."
- Ministry first, funds follow
- Multiple outreach-focused ministries

Rate your progress: 1   2   3   4   5   6   7   8   9   10

4. Gifted for Mission

Mission evolves from the spiritual gifts of individuals. People are no longer nominated to do tasks, but enabled to discern their gifts and use them for Christ. Volunteers do best what God has gifted them to do. They need to be coached, not controlled. Create a process of gifts discernment and an atmosphere of celebration for the ministries of all people.

FROM MAINTENANCE MINISTRY:
- People nominated to administrate
- Many supervise, few do ministry
- Membership goal: holding offices

TO EFFECTIVE MISSION
- People equipped to use their gifts
- Few supervise, many do ministry
- Membership goal: deepening faith journey

Rate your progress: 1   2   3   4   5   6   7   8   9   10

5. Train Lay Leaders

Equip the ministry of the laity. People yearn to make a difference difference because of the gospel. Clergy can train, motivate, and coach members. The church is moving from a pastor-centered "clergy-does-all" mindset to shared ministries of clergy and laity, continually upgrading for excellence.

FROM MAINTENANCE MINISTRY:
- Pastor takes care of people
- Clergy-control ministry
- "Merely a member"
- "Giving the best I have"
- Acceptance of mediocrity

TO EFFECTIVE MISSION
- People reach out to people
- Laity empowered to do ministry
- "Called to be a disciple of Christ"
- "Being the best I can be"
- Intention for quality

Rate your progress: 1   2   3   4   5   6   7   8   9   10

6. Called to Reach Out

Everyone is a potential guest seeking to be changed by the gospel. Don't expect unchurched people to seek out the church. Change the direction of your thinking—go to the people! Be zealous about hospitality; minister to your neighborhood. The natural direction for the gospel is outward. Inward-focused congregations never see mission beyond themselves and become like families addicted to their own needs.

FROM MAINTENANCE MINISTRY:
- Inward-looking
- Caring for own needs
- People united to do one thing
- Concern for social issues
- Thought/discussion about faith
- Process: enroll, inform, nominate, supervise, maintain

TO EFFECTIVE MISSION
- Outward-focused
- Caring for the needs of others
- People dispersed to do many things
- Action to heal the broken and feed the hungry
- Active, engaged faith
- Process: invite, change, discover gifts, call to ministry, equip, send

Rate your progress: 1   2   3   4   5   6   7   8   9   10

"Eight Critical Shifts Worksheet," *The Reaching Congregations: Tips and Tools to Strengthen Intentional Outreach*, David Poling-Goldenne et al, ELCA, 1996.
Catching the Next Wave: Leadership Strategies for Turn-Around Congregations. Copyright © Augsburg Fortress. May be reproduced for local use.

7. Multiple Ways to Experience the Holy

The gospel is conveyed through many mediums and diverse experiences. Multiply the options of worship. Expand the communications vehicles; appeal to all the senses; aim at the heart, and transform a life. Become all things to all people in order to rescue some. Trust the ability of people to find their own way to celebrate and share God's life-changing power.

FROM MAINTENANCE MINISTRY:	TO EFFECTIVE MISSION
Single type of worship	Diverse types of worship
Print-only worship	Multimedia worship
Mono-sound	Surround-sound
One point of entry	Many entry points
Verbal announcements	Interactive advertising
Homogeneous evangelism	Cross-cultural evangelism
Single generic outreach	Multiple designated missions

Rate your progress: 1   2   3   4   5   6   7   8   9   10

8. Profound, Relevant Theology

Ground leadership and ministries in the living Word of God. Connect the principles of faith with the practicalities of living, and interpret doctrines and liturgies in understandable and relevant language. Move beyond abstract truth to proclaim a gospel that liberates people from destructive addictions. Help seekers answer the question "Why does this make a difference to me?" and ask, "Would an unchurched person feel welcome and understand this event?"

FROM MAINTENANCE MINISTRY:	TO EFFECTIVE MISSION
Theological words	Complex words defined with meaning
Intellectual lectures	Communication targeted for the "heart"
Biblical information	Biblical words with the intent to transform
Expository sermons	Mentoring messages
Preaching primarily for members	Teaching that anticipates presence of unchurched

Rate your progress: 1   2   3   4   5   6   7   8   9   10

Summary questions
✔ What insights did we gain from this assessment tool?
✔ How is our congregation focused on maintenance?
✔ How is our congregation focused on mission?
✔ What attitudes exist in our congregation that may hamper a focus on mission?
✔ How can these attitudes be changed?

VISION TEAM: Compile responses for use in the plan phase. What were the differences, if any, between the data from the vision team and from the congregation groups? What might account for these differences?

KINDLING A SHARED VISION

How do 100, 350, or 4,000 individuals simultaneously detect the same vision from God in order to move forward in faith (*Catching the Next Wave*, pp. 75–76)? This is the next challenge for the vision team. The following worksheets can help the team facilitate the congregation's discussions in such a way that it arrives at a God-inspired shared vision.

> **Unanimity is rare.**
> Waiting for total consensus is disaster!
>
> *Catching the Next Wave*, p. 79

Three Stages Leading to a Shared Vision

Stage 1: Discussion

In this stage the congregation discusses the different levels of vision (see p. 52) and determines the level that they will plan to achieve. Data from the study phase of the turn-around process may indicate initial ideas about God's vision. Identifying common threads in the data through discussion gives further guidance. Using the APA Brainstorming Technique and the Scenario Planning Model, clarify the data (see p. 53).

VISION TEAM PLANNING

Pray! How many meetings will be needed? Who will conduct meetings? Is the data in presentable form? What Bible studies are needed for guidance, direction, and focus? Who will be invited to attend these meetings? What meeting formats will we use? How will we use the levels of vision study sheet (p. 52)? Who might help us with working through old issues of vision?

NOTES

_____

_____

_____

_____

_____

Stage 2: Deliberation

This phase has the congregation reviewing and thinking about the scenarios developed previously. At this time, it is appropriate to give the congregation a variety of activities and methods by which to strengthen its trust and guide its thoughts. Intentional corporate and individual prayer throughout this process is vital. Bible studies and small group discussions help individuals see God's vision for the lost. Over a period, the vision team assembles a scenario that emerges as a common understanding. Once refined, this vision is then presented to the congregation.

VISION TEAM PLANNING

Keep praying! Check the church calendar. What other activities are going on that might conflict or overshadow this process? What written and verbal communication forms will be utilized? How long might this process take? Which scenarios meet God's mission in your community? Who will sort through the scenarios to lift up the strongest? Who might help the vision team clarify the scenarios: separate task group, member of vision team, member of governing board?

NOTES

_____

_____

_____

> **Prayer during deliberation—try these!**
>
> ☐ Congregation-wide day of prayer and fasting
>
> ☐ Round-the-clock prayer vigil
>
> ☐ New or existing prayer teams
>
> ☐ Prayer in existing small groups and classes
>
> ☐ Corporate prayer in worship

> **Criteria for testing scenarios:**
> How well does this scenario serve God's reconciling mission to the lost and lonely in our world? See Col.1:20.

Stage 3: Decision

This is the most difficult stage of establishing a shared vision. Present the clarified vision to the congregation. "The key element to congregational decisions lies in deciding beforehand how to decide" (*Catching the Next Wave*, p. 79). The best decision-making process avoids a formal vote and creates a spontaneous burst of commitment. A graduated form of balloting may be used as well as a trial period for the new vision. Do not expect 100 percent acceptance. Use sensitivity and grace, but move toward making the vision come alive.

VISION TEAM PLANNING

Allow the scenarios to be reviewed by as many people in the congregation as possible. How will the vision team accomplish this? Is the congregation ready to decide or do they need more time? Is one scenario surfacing as the shared vision? Should our congregation provide a trial period for the scenario(s)?

NOTES

_____

_____

_____

> **No spontaneous burst of commitment? Try this:**
>
> ☐ State scenario clearly.
>
> ☐ Vote.
>
>   — If the vote results in less than 60% consensus for the vision, continue the deliberation.
>
>   — If the vote is more than 60% but less than 75%, implement the vision on a trial basis.
>
>   — If the vote results in more than 75% consensus, accept the vision!

Three Levels of Vision

VISION TEAM: It is important for the congregation to understand the difference between mission and vision and to understand the different levels of vision. Utilize this discussion sheet with your group. Develop examples of each type of vision from those that were or may be operating in your congregation. When this subject is discussed, these examples may uncover old hurts and issues. Stop and deal with the issues before continuing. Show compassion and understanding but use the opportunity to teach. If the issues become divisive, utilize members in your congregation with gifts for facilitating group discussions, processing tensions, and resolving conflict. For more serious conflicts, seek outside help.

> Only a vivid mental picture of the future God desires, shared among the majority of the membership, will propel the congregation through its status quo.
>
> *Catching the Next Wave*, p. 71

Low
Competing vision

This is the lowest and most common level of vision. In this level there are shared visions but different groups have different visions that are exclusive of each other. No one is willing to give theirs up, so the visions "compete."

Middle
Cooperative vision

In this middle ground level there are multiple visions, but groups are willing to negotiate and come to an agreement. Groups compromise some of their visions to maintain harmony and please a majority. The final agreed-upon vision is different than previously desired by any group.

High
Supraordinate vision

This level of vision transcends the lower two levels and has all members united in one vision for ministry. Members have let go of their own desires, natural competitions, and compromises to unite in a vision that serves God through them and their congregation.

Discussion questions
- In what way have you experienced any of these levels of vision?
- Discuss examples shared.
- Discuss the benefits of cooperative vision. What are the disadvantages?
- What would be the preferred level for vision in your congregation? Why?

Techniques for Creating a Shared Vision

VISION TEAM: These techniques are useful in the discussion stage of creating a shared vision. Study these techniques and understand them before using them with the congregation. As an exercise, try the process with the vision team first. What are some of the potential scenarios the vision team sees as possible? Will additional information be needed? What is the best way to set up this type of meeting? Who should be present to help the process flow?

APA Brainstorming Technique: Achieve, Protect, and Avoid

GOAL: To discern potential visions by listing everything the congregation hopes to achieve, protect, or avoid

STEP 1: The facilitator has the assembled group categorize the "common threads" identified in the study phase into three categories: those things the congregation wants to achieve, protect, and avoid. Lists are generated and recorded on flipcharts, then are posted on the wall for all to see.

STEP 2: New ideas are generated through brainstorming and added to the APA lists. This means all ideas are shared without evaluating or judging.

STEP 3: Once all the ideas have been shared and posted, the group begins to identify common threads in the data.

STEP 4: Use the Scenario Planning Method to put this data in useful form.

> **Planning checklist**
> - [ ] Who has the skills to facilitate this meeting and process? A vision team member or someone else?
> - [ ] What form should the study phase data be in to facilitate discussion?
> - [ ] Should we break into small groups by category or stay in one group? Other format?
> - [ ] Do we need to plan multiple meetings, or can we complete the discussion stage in one meeting?

Scenario Planning Method

GOAL: To create complete, imaginative depictions of potential futures for the congregation.

STEP 1: Use the common threads identified by the APA technique to assemble scenarios. Make each scenario as vivid as possible with the congregation envisioning what the future would look like in each depiction.

STEP 2: Then stop group discussion and refrain from choosing a preferred scenario. Time should be spent communicating these scenarios to the entire congregation for review and deliberation. This takes time and patience but allows the end result to belong to all the people and not one small group of members.

STEP 3: Clarify the scenarios by listening to feedback from the congregation.

> **Planning questions**
> - [ ] How do we communicate these scenarios to the congregation?
> - [ ] What system do we want to establish for gathering reactions and opinions? Interviews, written forms, telephone contact?
> - [ ] How will we process reactions and clarify and report selections?
> - [ ] How will we test these visions to determine which one is of God?

For additional information, see *Catching the Next Wave: Leadership Strategies for Turn-Around Congregations*, Chapter 6, "Kindling a Shared Vision."

GROUP DEVELOPMENT OF A SHARED VISION

VISION TEAM: You are making progress! It is now time to think about organizing to create a shared vision. Much time has been spent in the study phase. Thorough planning as you start the plan phase is imperative. Consider these items:

Vision Team Checklist

☐ Who will be invited to participate?

_____

_____

☐ Who will lead this process?

_____

_____

☐ How many participants will be invited?

_____

_____

☐ How many meetings will we need?

_____

_____

☐ How long should each meeting be?

_____

_____

☐ What Bible studies will we use?
(See pages 76–80.)

_____

_____

☐ What meeting formats might we use:
overnight or weekend retreats, morning,
afternoon, or evening meetings?

_____

_____

☐ How will we handle a trial stage?

_____

_____

Sample Agenda Content and Schedule of Meetings

MEETING 1:
- ☐ Begin with prayer and Bible study.
- ☐ Review mission.
- ☐ Define vision.
- ☐ Study levels of vision.
- ☐ Discuss three-part process for creating a shared vision.
- ☐ Sensing no conflict resolution is needed, move to meeting 2.

_____

_____

_____

MEETING 2:
- ☐ Begin with prayer and Bible study.
- ☐ Review meeting 1.
- ☐ Review material from study phase.
- ☐ Use APA Brainstorming Technique to sort data.
- ☐ Continue or go to meeting 3.

_____

_____

_____

MEETING 3:
- ☐ Begin with prayer and Bible study.
- ☐ Review meeting 2.
- ☐ Discuss Scenario Planning Method.
- ☐ Complete scenarios.
- ☐ Disband group for deliberation stage.

_____

_____

_____

MEETING 4:
- ☐ Begin with prayer and Bible study.
- ☐ Review meeting 3.
- ☐ Clarify scenarios.
- ☐ Accept by spontaneous commitment or graduated voting.
- ☐ Plan presentation to congregation.

_____

_____

_____

MISSION STRATEGIES: ORGANIZATION

VISION **T**EAM: The inventory "Is Our Congregation Healthy?" on pages 6–8 of this workbook is a useful tool for the plan stage. Or use the data from the completed inventory to help focus on congregational organization.

STEP 1: How is your congregation organized for mission?

Every living organism has structure. A congregation needs structure that is clearly defined and supports mission.

Discussion questions
- How is our congregation organized?
- How is our governing board organized?
- How are decisions made?

- What types of groups are functioning well?
- What groups are not functioning well?
- Why might this difference exist?
- How many people are involved in active ministry?

STEP 2: Clarify volunteerism in your congregation.

EXERCISE **1:** *Define volunteerism in your congregation.*

Discussion questions
- How are volunteers recruited?
- How long do volunteers stay in a group?
- Do volunteers leave before a task is completed? Why?
- What types of activities receive the most participation? Why?

EXERCISE **2:** *Study this emerging definition of volunteerism.*

In today's world, volunteers look for short-term commitments that have a beginning and an end. These commitments need clear expectations and provide direct hands-on ministry opportunities that exhibit tangible results.

Discussion questions
- What kinds of groups and tasks does our congregation provide?
- What time commitments are required of volunteers?
- How do people know what they are volunteering to do?
- When are results of tasks and service opportunities possible or available?
- How much time is spent making decisions versus making ministry happen?
- How long are governing board meetings?
- What does this new definition of volunteerism mean to our congregation?

STEP 3: Review new methods for organizing your congregation for ministry in today's world.

Method 1: Team Ministry

Team ministry is lay volunteers and church professionals sharing a common mission and vision, released from bureaucracies and strengthened by their unique gifts and talents to accomplish the work God has called them to do.

EXERCISE 1: *Review the following information and answer the discussion questions.*

The term *team* usually is associated with a group of people getting a task done. A church that organizes around teams actually develops a teaming culture. Prince of Peace Lutheran Church, Burnsville, Minn., identifies five principles to a congregational teaming culture:

- The basic work unit is a *team*. A structure with teams allows gifts, relationships, and mission to take priority over running the church. Instead of reporting to the top of the organization, teams form webs of interactions and do ministry.

- There is a shared mission and vision. *Mission* is God's calling and brings loyalty to the team. *Vision* gives specific direction to the team on how to accomplish God's mission.

- Teams operate with mutual trust and accountability. The mission and the vision of the congregation guides all teams and everything each team strives to accomplish. A basic trust in this fact is required for a healthy team. Accountability is based on leaders relinquishing control and believing "we can do it together."

- Teams focus on giftedness. Spiritual gifts are God's plan for building the church. Each team is composed of people with a variety of gifts that make ministry happen.

- Teaming fosters systems thinking. Each team is fully aware and functions knowing that it is a piece of the whole. All teams work for the good of the entire organism, the congregation.

Adapted from *Changing Church Perspectives*, April/June and August/September 1998, Teri Elton.

Discussion questions
- How do teams differ from committees?
- What level of trust does our congregation extend to various groups?
- How does our congregation affirm spiritual gifts?

EXERCISE 2: *Is team ministry for our congregation?*

Establishing a teaming culture in a congregation requires a new way of thinking. Bill Easum, author and church consultant, defines this new method of thinking and operating as "permission giving." Consider these basic characteristics of permission-giving churches and determine your congregation's readiness for team ministry:

WE DO / WE CAN / WE WON'T

- ☐ ☐ ☐ Permission-giving churches believe that the role of God's people is to minister to people, not to serve on committees and make decisions about what can or cannot be done.

- ☐ ☐ ☐ Permission-giving churches encourage decisions to be made not by board members, leaders, or staff, but by people engaged in the ministry.

- ☐ ☐ ☐ Permission-giving churches encourage ministry to happen wherever there is a need.

- ☐ ☐ ☐ Permission-giving churches have leaders who intentionally equip and release people into ministry, affirming their spiritual gifts.

- ☐ ☐ ☐ Permission-giving churches replace vertical hierarchies with horizontal networks that are flexible.

- ☐ ☐ ☐ Permission-giving churches provide accountability through mission, vision, and a solid set of corporate values.

Scoring: If most checks are in the first two columns, begin to consider how team ministry may be implemented in your congregation. If there are any checks in the third column, discuss why you feel this practice is not possible in your congregation and consider how these conclusions will affect your mission and vision.

Sacred Cows Make Gourmet Hamburgers, Abingdon Press, Bill Easum, 1995; pp. 51–55.

EXERCISE 3: *To begin developing a team ministry, complete the items on this checklist.*

☐ Pray.

☐ Design a team ministry that is uniquely yours.

☐ Identify the areas that require ministry teams to exist. These are core ministries.

☐ Allow a significant amount of time to make the transition to team ministry. Plan changes in stages over a period of two to four years.

☐ Determine how teams will receive training and the information necessary to operate.

☐ Identify which areas of ministry are to be modified to support teams.

☐ Identify the order in which existing systems are transitioned to teams.

☐ Establish accountability guidelines.

_____

_____

_____

_____

_____

_____

_____

Sacred Cows Make Gourmet Hamburgers, Abingdon Press, Bill Easum, 1995; pp. 129, 170–172.

Method 2: Governing Board and Staff Structure

Exercise 1. *Reflect on the description from Step 1 (p. 56) which identifies the way your congregation is organized for ministry. Focus on the congregation's governing board by reviewing the results of the following inventory describing characteristics of a healthy congregation board.*

ALWAYS USUALLY SOMETIMES NEVER

☐ ☐ ☐ ☐   People are excited and honored to serve on the congregation board.

☐ ☐ ☐ ☐   Every meeting begins with prayer.

☐ ☐ ☐ ☐   Every meeting includes biblical reflection.

☐ ☐ ☐ ☐   Agendas are flexible but concise.

☐ ☐ ☐ ☐   The board spends time visioning for the future.

☐ ☐ ☐ ☐   The board does not micromanage the work of other groups.

☐ ☐ ☐ ☐   Meetings last from 90 minutes to two hour maximum.

☐ ☐ ☐ ☐   Board members display positive attitudes.

☐ ☐ ☐ ☐   Members are willing to take risks and try new strategies to grow ministry.

☐ ☐ ☐ ☐   Decisions are made based on the mission and vision of the congregation.

☐ ☐ ☐ ☐   The board has between 9 and 12 participants for streamlined decision making.

☐ ☐ ☐ ☐   Every meeting closes with prayer.

Discussion questions

✔ What are the strengths of our board?

✔ Where are the weaknesses of our board?

✔ What changes are necessary to become more effective?

EXERCISE 2: *Review the following scenario. Use the discussion questions to identify areas of interest to you.*

Scenario: Governing board as a board of directors. In this format, the council meets for 90 minutes total. The time is divided into three 30-minute segments: prayer and biblical reflection, business, and visioning. When a segment goes over, recontract for 15-minute slots, or table the remainder of segment to the next meeting. The business segment addresses action items on reports submitted by staff or teams that have been read in advance. The visioning segment is planned by the staff, or is predetermined at an annual board planning session for the coming year. The meeting closes with the sharing of concerns and prayer. Prayer for each other and for congregational concerns is encouraged between meetings.

Discussion questions
- What is appealing about this scenario?
- What seems impossible for our congregation to accomplish? Why?
- How might this format be adapted to work in our congregation?
- What pieces of this format might we try in our congregation?

_____
_____
_____
_____
_____
_____

EXERCISE 3: *Review the following trends in staffing. How might these work in your congregation? How might you adapt these options?*

STAFF-LED MINISTRY TEAMS: In today's busy culture, volunteers do not want to spend what spare time they have coordinating activities. Consider a part-time staff person to oversee the business in a designated area for ministry and release participants to do ministry. Sample areas of ministry: adult, youth, family ministries, worship, evangelism, and administration.

CLERGY AND LAY PROFESSIONALS IN TEAM MINISTRY: Congregations are finding it more productive and economical to hire lay professionals to complement a pastor's leadership role. The clergy generalist is being replaced by an ordained person who has knowledge and leadership skills to reach people through Word and Sacrament. Lay-professional specialists cover areas such as administration, small groups, and membership integration.

FULL-TIME STAFF TO PART-TIME STAFF: One full-time position can be divided into several smaller positions and filled with part-time staff. This multiplies ministries and people involved in those ministries. For example, a music director can be replaced with three positions covering worship, vocal/bell choirs, and instruments/band. A full-time ordained minister of pastoral care position may become a prayer ministry leader, caring and listening ministry leader, and a church nurse.

"Changing Staff Configurations," Lyle Schaller, *Net Results*, Sept. 1997.

TIP! Can't afford a part-time person? Consider an employee for ten hours a week. Provide a job description, and give staff status and recognition. Call the position "coordinator" (for adult ministry, worship, finances) or another title. Lift people out of the congregation with the passion and gifts for this ministry. Starting this way identifies people who want to develop ministry, and sets the stage for growing that staff position in the future.

Realigning a congregation's organization structure more than once every decade will create the illusion of progress, while producing confusion, inefficiency, and demoralization (*Catching the Next Wave*, p. 86).

Sidebar labels: HEALTH · DESIGN · STUDY · PLAN · ACT · TEND

MISSION STRATEGIES: GROWTH

Growth, the second criteria for healthy congregations, distinguishes living things from all nonliving things.

VISION TEAM: Use this checklist for vision team review first and then with congregational discussion groups. Read the material on pages 60–63 and prepare handouts or overheads. Form small groups for discussion of questions.

> ### Vision team checklist
>
> ☐ Who will lead these discussions?
>
> ☐ Which inventories will we use?
>
> ☐ How will this material be used with other groups?
>
> ☐ Who will do additional research with recommended resources?
>
> ☐ How will additional resource material be shared?

STEP 1:
What is happening in our world today?

EXERCISE 1:
Lyman Coleman, author and proponent of small-group ministries, lists the following three social changes that have significantly impacted people today:

- Gone are safe neighborhoods.
- Gone are secure jobs.
- Gone are local, extended family.

Discussion questions
- Which of these statements has impacted our congregation? Community?
- How have these situations affected our congregation? Community?
- What ministries has our congregation developed to meet these needs in our congregation? Community?

EXERCISE 2:
In addition, a Gallup poll sites the following top six basic needs of people not being met by American churches. Those needs are to:

- Believe life is meaningful and has purpose.
- Have a sense of community and deeper relationships.
- Be appreciated and respected.
- Be listened to and heard.
- Feel that they are growing in faith.
- Have practical help in developing a mature faith.

Discussion questions
- What ministries in our congregation meet these needs?
- Where might the breakdown be between congregation and those who feel their needs are not being met?
- What new ministries might address these basic needs?

STEP 2:
Review methods for growing your congregation.

Invitational Evangelism Emphasis

VISION TEAM: Review this information in your team meetings. Then use with congregational discussion groups for identifying evangelism strategies that would help your congregation grow.

■ *"Invitation is what evangelism is all about! It is one person inviting another to find the Lord"* (Martin Marty).

Invitation evangelism works! Key studies confirm the value of a strong emphasis on equipping members to invite and share. Consider the following and use the discussion questions to gather insight about your congregation.

■ *"Word of mouth and other people contacts were the primary reasons given for 'shopping' or visiting a new congregation"* (Church Membership Initiative, 1993).

■ *"Eighty-one percent of their members invites one other person to come to church with them each year; 60 percent invite three or more; an incredible 28.8 percent invite eight or more people each year"* (Study of Community Lutheran Church conducted by students at the University of Nevada-Las Vegas).

■ In a survey that asked 21,000 people how they came to Christ and the church, 75 percent to 95 percent said they were invited by a friend or relative (Win Arn).

Discussion questions
✔ What does this information mean to our congregation?
✔ How can our congregation be more invitational to friends, relatives, coworkers, or unchurched people in the community?
✔ What mission strategies would focus our mission on invitational evangelism?

—Selections from *Friendship Sunday Planning Guide*, Raymond D. Christenson and David Poling-Goldenne, Evangelical Lutheran Church in America, 1994, p. 8.

Growth Strategies to Explore

☐ Host a Friendship Sunday.

☐ Host a revival.

☐ Host a Christmas or Easter pageant open to the community, and provide tickets for members to share with their neighbors.

☐ Plan the development of a neighborhood kids' club.

☐ Host vacation Bible school and summer day camp, and follow up with invitations issued to new families.

☐ Begin to reach out cross-culturally to neighbors of different ethnic backgrounds.

☐ Consider starting a school. Contact denominational offices for guidance and resources.

☐ Follow up with visitors to worship.

☐ Design a Web site.

☐ Develop an outreach newsletter.

☐ Go door-to-door in your community to talk with residents.

☐ Plan a new worship service for a population of residents not currently being reached by any church.

Resources for Growth

Brandt, Donald M., *Worship and Outreach: New Services for New People*, Augsburg Fortress, 1994.

Poling-Goldenne, David, et al, *Making Christ Known: A Guide to Evangelism for Congregations*, Augsburg Fortress, 1996.

Poling-Goldenne, Marta, *Evangelism Essentials: An Assessment Tool*, Evangelical Lutheran Church in America, 1998.

Sorensen, Paul, *Sharing Your Faith with Friends, Relatives, and Neighbors*, Augsburg Fortress, 1995.

Wollersheim, Gary, *Preparing Lay Callers for Community Outreach*, Augsburg Fortress, 1995.

Go to www.elca.org/eteam for evangelism resources that can be downloaded.

STEP 3:
Explore small-group ministry as a way to reach and disciple new people.

EXERCISE 1: *Read these definitions of small groups and answer the discussion questions.*

"A Christian small group is an intentional face to face gathering of 3 to 12 people on a regular time schedule with the common purpose of discovery and growing in the possibilities of the abundant life in Christ" (Roberta Hestenes, *Building Christian Community through Small Groups*, p. 27).

A small group is the primary place where people can be reconstructed, equipped, and released for God's work in a broken world (Lyman Coleman, author and founder of Serendipity House).

Discussion questions
- How do these definitions of small groups apply to the three social changes noted in Exercise 1 on page 60?
- How do these definitions address the basic needs of people as listed in the Gallup poll?
- How would small-group ministry help our congregation grow?

EXERCISE 2: *Are small groups needed in your church?*

VISION TEAM: Complete this assessment. Use with a group for assessing congregational needs for small groups.

YES	NO	
☐	☐	Are church members seeking to better understand how the Bible applies to their life situations?
☐	☐	Has the work of the committees become a chore rather than a blessing?
☐	☐	Do members indicate a need for opportunities to identify, use, and further develop their spiritual gifts?
☐	☐	Do members and potential members indicate a need for opportunities to connect with each other?

YES	NO	
☐	☐	Do members seek opportunities outside of worship to hear and receive God's grace?
☐	☐	Is there a need to develop leaders in your church?
☐	☐	Has your membership failed to increase in numbers for several years due to members leaving or moving into inactivity?
☐	☐	Is your church searching for new ways to retain members and reach inactives?
☐	☐	Does your church have a commitment to reaching people who are unchurched?

EXERCISE 3: *Identify types of small groups.*

VISION TEAM: There are many models for small-group ministries. Your congregation will need to study the type of ministry that will help your congregation grow. For a complete resource on developing small groups, refer to *Starting Small Groups and Keeping Them Going* (Augsburg Fortress, 1995). Use the basic information on the following page to study as a potential mission strategy.

Types of Small Groups

DISCIPLESHIP GROUPS
This type of small group focuses on biblical reflection. Examples include a Bible study or topical book study related to a faith issue.

SUPPORT AND RECOVERY GROUPS
This type of group focuses on specific issues such as parenting or a Christian 12-step group for addiction recovery. These groups are most effective at involving unchurched people.

MINISTRY GROUPS
This type of group is focused more on a task and includes committees and task groups.

Four Essential Components of Small Groups

PRAYER
Growing closer to God and to each other by praying for and with each other in a variety of ways is central to a healthy small group.

BIBLICAL REFLECTION
This component focuses on God's word through reflection and study of a biblical text. The goal of the study is to relate the insights to one's daily journey of faith.

MUTUAL SUPPORT
Learning to listen to each other by sharing stories and providing care helps participants to discover the value of building community.

GROUP MINISTRY TASK
We are blessed to be a blessing! A group learns accountability as participants take on specific tasks to serve their church or the wider community. This component helps to prevent cliques from forming.

From *Starting Small Groups and Keeping Them Going*, Augsburg Fortress, 1995, p. 17.

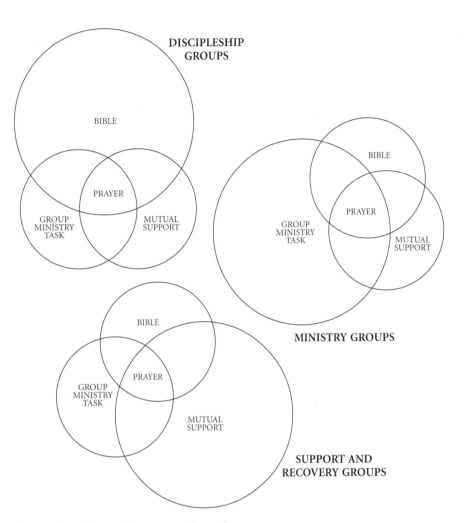

Organizational Approaches to Small-Group Ministries in Your Congregation

SPECIALIZED APPROACH
A specialized, intentional ministry of small groups is one that is added to the existing structure of your congregation. For example, support groups are developed and added as a program ministry to address a specific need.

INTEGRATED APPROACH
An integrated, intentional model of small groups includes developing new small groups as needed and assisting existing groups like committees, teams, and governing boards to use the same four essential components. This approach takes more time to implement than the specialized approach.

From *Starting Small Groups and Keeping Them Going*, Augsburg Fortress, 1995, p. 14.

Discussion questions
- ✔ What groups are now operating in our congregation that look something like these groups? How might they benefit from incorporating the four essential components?
- ✔ What new groups might be helpful to meet the needs of our congregation? Community?
- ✔ How might existing groups benefit from this organizational model?
- ✔ What additional research is needed?

MISSION STRATEGIES: MOVEMENT

Movement generates energy and momentum" (*Catching the Next Wave*, p. 8).

The following resources provide how-to ideas and mission strategies for creating, maintaining, and further developing a healthy turn-around momentum. Also see the resources mentioned in the bibliography in *Catching the Next Wave: Leadership Strategies for Turn-Around Congregations.*

> **Healthy self-esteem** builds with successful first steps. Momentum grows with genuine enthusiasm. Confidence accelerates through prayer and faith.

Books for Foundational Planning

Bandy, Thomas G., *Moving Off the Map: A Field Guide to Changing the Congregation*, Abingdon Press, 1998.

Capers, James M., *African American Evangelism: Proclaiming the Power*, Augsburg Fortress, 1996.

Capers, James M., *Planning Revivals in African American Contexts*, Augsburg Fortress, 1993.

Easum, William M. and Bandy, Thomas G., *Growing Spiritual Redwoods*, Abingdon Press, 1997.

Easum, William M., *Dancing with Dinosaurs: Ministry in a Hostile and Hurting World*, Abingdon Press, 1993.

Easum, William M., *The Church Growth Handbook*, Abingdon Press, 1990.

Easum, William M., *The Complete Ministry Audit: How to Measure 20 Principles for Growth*, Abingdon Press, 1996 (spreadsheet disk included).

Easum, William M., *Sacred Cows Make Gourmet Burgers*, Abingdon Press, 1995.

Kallestad, Walt and Schey, Steve, *Total Quality Ministry*, Augsburg Fortress, 1994.

Ruffcorn, Kevin, *Rural Evangelism: Catching the Vision*, Augsburg Fortress, 1994.

Schaller, Lyle E., *Strategies for Change*, Abingdon Press, 1993.

Schey, Stephen L. and Kallestad, Walt, *Team Ministry: A Workbook for Getting Things Done*, Abingdon Press, 1996.

Strommen, Merton P., *The Innovative Church: Seven Steps to Positive Change in Your Congregation*, Augsburg Fortress, 1997.

Villa, George, *Evangelización en la Comunidad: Una Guia para la Congregación*, Augsburg Fortress, 1994.

Warren, Rick, *The Purpose-Driven Church: Growth without Compromising Your Message*, Zondervan, 1995.

Books for Leadership Development

George, Carl F. (with Warren Bird), *Nine Keys to Effective Small Group Leadership*, Kingdom, 1997.

Harbaugh, Gary L., *God's Gifted People*, Augsburg Fortress, 1990.

Harris, Lee W., *Effective Church Leadership: A Practical Sourcebook*, Augsburg Fortress, 1989.

Neuchterlein, Ann Marie, *Improving Your Multiple Staff Ministry: How to Work Together More Effectively*, Augsburg Fortress, 1989.

Towns, Elmer, *The Eight Laws of Leadership: Making Extraordinary Leaders out of Ordinary Believers*, Church Growth Institute, 1992.

Books for "Coloring Outside the Lines"

Kallestad, Walt, *Entertainment Evangelism: Taking the Church Public*, Abingdon Press, 1996.

Mcintosh, Gary, *Three Generations*, Fleming H. Revell Publishing, 1995.

Popcorn, Faith. and Marigold, Lys, *Clicking: 17 Trends That Drive Your Business and Your Life*, Harper Business, 1997.

Towns, Elmer L., *Ten of Today's Most Innovative Churches*, Regal Books, 1990.

What Next? Connecting Your Ministry with the Generation Formerly Known as X, Augsburg Fortress, 1999.

Resources for Making Disciples

Bose, Neal and Haller, Patricia, "Opening Your Spiritual Gifts," ELCA, 1995.

Haller, Patricia A., *Make New Members Active Members*, Augsburg Fortress, 1995.

Marty, Martin, *Come and Grow with Us: New Member Basics*, Augsburg Fortress, 1996.

Schmalenberger, Jerry, "Invitation to Discipleship: A Quick Reader for Spiritual Seekers," ELCA, 1995.

Smith, James Bryan, *A Spiritual Formation Workbook*, Harper San Francisco, 1993.

Smith, Patricia Liles, *Come and Grow with Us: New Member Basics, Leader Guide*, Augsburg Fortress, 1996.

Trumbauer, Jean Morris, *Sharing the Ministry: A Practical Guide for Transforming Volunteers into Ministers*, and *Discovering the Gifts of the People* (a gifts inventory that accompanies *Sharing the Ministry*), Augsburg Fortress, 1995.

Welcome to Christ: A Lutheran Catechetical Guide, Augsburg Fortress, 1997.

Welcome to Christ: A Lutheran Introduction to the Catechumenate, Augsburg Fortress, 1997.

Welcome to Christ: Lutheran Rites for the Catechumenate, Augsburg Fortress, 1997.

"Do It Yourself" Video Seminars

Awakening: Hospitality Evangelism, Division for Congregational Ministries, ELCA, 1994.

Choices: New Concepts for Ministry in The 21st Century, Division for Congregational Ministries, ELCA, 1996.

Counting Your Community: Using Census Statistics as Part of Congregational Planning, Division for Congregational Ministries, ELCA, 1996.

Disciple: Strategies to Help Congregations Call and Equip Christians to Reach Out and Transform Lives, Division for Congregational Ministries, ELCA, 1995.

Easum, William M., *The Permission-Giving Church: Sacred Cows Make Gourmet Hamburgers*, 21st Century Strategies, Inc, 1997.

Faith! Living It. Sharing It! Division for Congregational Ministries, ELCA, 1998.

Go Public: Designing Radio Ministry for Communication Evangelism, Department for Communication, ELCA, (audiotape and CD), 1997.

Go Public: Motivating Your Congregation for Communication Evangelism, Division for Congregational Ministries, ELCA, 1997.

Kallestad, Walt, and Tim Wright, *Reaching the Unchurched: Creating the Vision*, Augsburg Fortress, 1994.

Renewed: Reinventing Rural Ministry, Division for Congregational Ministries, ELCA, 1995.

Restored: Portraits of and Strategies for Innovative, Urban Congregations, Division for Congregational Ministries, ELCA, 1996.

CD-ROM

Alive in Christ, ELCA, 1998. (A complete ministry planning resource with tips and helps for your congregational programs in Christian education, evangelism, worship, stewardship, social ministry, and more).

NOTE: Augsburg Fortress and ELCA resources in this listing may be ordered by calling (800) 328-4648.

HEALTH

DESIGN

STUDY

PLAN

ACT

TEND

MISSION STRATEGIES: TRANSFORMATION

Healthy congregations serve the gospel by being communities where faith transforms individual members (*Catching the Next Wave*, p. 9).

VISION TEAM: Use the evaluation tool, "Is Our Congregation Healthy?" (p. 6), as a group activity. Consider the following ideas for growing a stronger prayer life in your congregation.

EXERCISE: *Choose one item in each level and discuss a possible plan for implementation considering leadership, scheduling, and communication.*

Resources for further study:

Beckman, Richard J., *Praying for Wholeness and Healing*, Augsburg Fortress, 1995.

Pedersen, Bjorn, *Face to Face with God in Your Church: Establishing a Prayer Ministry*, Augsburg Fortress, 1995.

Vennard, Jane E., *Praying for Friends and Enemies*, Augsburg Fortress, 1995.

Start Slow and Easy! Start-up Ministries

☐ **STAFF PRAYER:** A scheduled time, usually daily or weekly, is set aside by the church staff for praying together.

☐ **PRAYER CALENDAR:** A calendar identifying one or more prayer topics for each day of any given month or sequence of months is prepared and distributed.

☐ **PRAYER CHAIN:** A network of people who receive prayer requests over the telephone, pass the requests to others, and pray for each request.

☐ **NATIONAL DAY OF PRAYER:** Abraham Lincoln was the first president to designate the first Thursday in May as a day to pray for the United States of America. Form a prayer group for that day, send a representative to a city function, or publicize in your congregation newsletter and weekly worship folder.

Dig Deeper! Intermediate Ministries

☐ **PRAYER VIGIL:** A vigil provides a significant period of focused time for continuous prayer, usually on one specific topic.

☐ **PRAYER-EMPHASIS WEEK OR MONTH:** This is a period of time that is set aside by the congregation to reflect on the importance of prayer, to provide opportunities for prayer, and to invite God's spirit to make prayer more intentional for the entire congregation.

☐ **PRAYER CHAPEL:** This is a room in or near the sanctuary that is set aside for people who seek ministry through prayer following the worship service or at other designated times.

☐ **SMALL PRAYER GROUP:** This is a small group of people meeting in a home to learn about prayer and to pray.

Keep Going! Advanced Ministries

☐ **PRAYER TEAM:** This is a team of trained persons who meet in the prayer chapel before or after the worship service to pray with those who desire personal prayer.

☐ **PRAYER TELEPHONE MINISTRY:** This ministry allows people to receive prayer inspiration and/or support by telephone.

☐ **INTERCESSORY SUPPORT MINISTRY:** This is a team of intercessors who pray regularly at the request of a leader.

☐ **SCHOOL OR COLLEGE OF PRAYER:** This ministry offers courses about various aspects of prayer to encourage individual growth and development of leaders for specific prayer ministries.

Discussion questions

✔ What people resources do we have available?

✔ Which are appropriate first steps for our congregation?

REMEMBER! Think process; grow step by step!

MISSION STRATEGIES: SENSITIVITY

All living organisms need to be sensitive to their surroundings. "Plateaued and declining congregations that wish to turn around their downward spiral must relearn how to listen to their unchurched neighbors" (*Catching the Next Wave*, p. 90).

The following lists represent mission strategies to reach unchurched people:

Evangelism

☐ Share welcome packets with new residents.

☐ Host special events open to all: Easter egg hunt, garage sale, craft fair.

☐ Send special mailings for special occasions.

☐ Provide information about your congregation to local hotels, real estate agents, banks, and the Welcome Wagon.

☐ Engage in a publicity campaign in your community.

☐ Call on visitors to worship.

☐ Design educational youth activities and make them open to the public.

☐ Provide parenting classes, and publicize them in the community.

☐ Provide a nursery school, kindergarten, or day care.

☐ Host seminars according to need and interest; publicize and invite the community.

☐ Match up new members and visitors with mentors (established members).

☐ Develop an after-school program or a youth drop-in center.

☐ Develop a Parents' Night Out program for the community.

Community Outreach

☐ Distribute food, clothing, and other basic necessities to those in need.

☐ Offer senior care.

☐ Establish an adopt-a-grandparent program.

☐ Begin a Meals on Wheels program.

☐ Support a local shelter or feeding program.

☐ Host support groups, and publicize them to the community.

☐ Provide a Moms' Day Out program.

☐ Join a church-based community organizing group to advocate residents' needs for affordable housing, jobs, and community economic development.

☐ Host a community blood drive.

☐ Start a sports program for youth.

☐ Host a monthly or weekly professional luncheon with Bible study and prayer.

☐ Hold a community Bible study in a local restaurant.

☐ Provide literacy or English as a second language classes for neighborhood residents.

☐ Go door-to-door in the neighborhood to invite residents to a special event or worship service.

Worship and Outreach

☐ Offer multiple worship services.

☐ Offer choices in style of worship.

☐ Provide a user-friendly bulletin/worship folder and explain aloud how to use it.

☐ Have clear signs and directions to your church posted for visitors.

☐ Provide a special visitor parking area close to the sanctuary.

☐ Provide parking lot greeters.

☐ Provide clear instructions about receiving communion.

What ideas support your vision statement?

Wondering about who is unchurched? Try these!

- Interview newer members
- Door-to-door calling
- Review community statistics

—Adapted from *The Reaching Congregation—Tips and Tools to Strengthen Intentional Outreach*, David Poling-Goldenne, et al, ELCA, pp. 10–11.

HEALTH
DESIGN
STUDY
PLAN
ACT
TEND

MISSION STRATEGIES: ADAPTATION

Living organisms adapt to their surroundings. In this world of numerous choices, the church finds itself evaluating how best to reach more people with the good news of Jesus Christ through the experience of worship. "Multiple services in varying styles and music can make a significant contribution to a congregational turn around" (*Catching the Next Wave*, p. 92).

VISION TEAM: It is important to remember that each congregation uses similar terms for worship styles but frequently using different definitions. Review and discuss the following generalized options of different styles of worship:

CONTEMPORARY OPTION
This option has music that is currently popular, easy to memorize, and easy to sing. Often, easy-to-read worship folders have the entire service written out, or there is overhead projection of the service format. The organ is replaced with a band or keyboard. The choir is replaced with worship leaders and/or singers. The sermon is sensitive to people who are possibly biblically illiterate.

TRADITIONAL OPTION
This service follows denominational tradition and guidelines, often using a standard worship book. Most often, the primary musical instrument is the organ, and music is classical and from a well-developed heritage. Choirs also support this service style.

BLENDED OPTION
Combine elements of the contemporary and traditional options and you have a blended style. The challenge is to use different musical styles without making the service appear incongruous.

ETHNIC-SPECIFIC OPTION
For this option, research the musical styles offered in churches with the specific racial/ethnic group you desire to reach. Be intentional, respectful, and faithful.

Adapted from *Worship and Outreach: New Services for New People*, Donald M. Brandt, Augsburg Fortress, 1994.

Key question

What is the congregation's greatest potential for singing the heart song of the community in glory and praise to God?

Implementing a new service? Try these tips!

☐ Repeatedly share the reason for this new service, which is to reach new people.

☐ Involve as many people as possible in support roles for this new service.

☐ Do not disrupt existing services—add a new one.

☐ Affirm each style of worship.

Will having multiple or different styles of worship promote disunity? Not if . . .

☐ The pastor actively supports all services.

☐ The congregation wants to reach new people.

☐ The congregation appreciates variety.

☐ Worship has integrity and is done well in all areas.

Discussion questions

✔ How will multiple or different worship styles support the vision of our congregation?

✔ What new worship style would reach our community?

✔ What resources will we need to study and plan this mission strategy?

✔ How is the congregation ready for this kind of change?

MISSION STRATEGIES: REPRODUCTION

L iving organisms reproduce themselves. The church is called to reproduce disciples. "A mission strategy that seeks to place renewed importance on active discipleship of youth as well as new believers is essential to the reproductive health of a congregation" (*Catching the Next Wave*, p. 93).

Exercise 1

VISION TEAM: Use the following inventory as a discussion starter for understanding the need to reach young people with the love of Jesus Christ.

AGREE DISAGREE

☐ ☐ Many adults no longer consider it their responsibility to play a role in the lives of children outside their nuclear family.

☐ ☐ Parents are less available for their children because of demands outside the home and the cultural norms that undervalue parenting.

☐ ☐ Society has become age segregated, providing fewer opportunities for meaningful intergenerational relationships.

☐ ☐ The mass media has become influential shapers of young people's attitudes, norms, and values.

☐ ☐ As problems and solutions have become more complex, more responsibility for young people has been turned over to professionals.

From *Take It to Heart*, by Miriam Campbell Dumke, Evangelical Lutheran Church in America and Lutheran Brotherhood, 1998, p. 14.

Discussion questions
✔ What examples of each statement in the inventory can we name (Exercise 1)?

✔ Which statements provide opportunities for our church to reach out to young people (Exercise 1)?

✔ What strategies match the gifts and vision of our congregation (Exercise 2)?

Exercise 2

Review the following strategies for reaching out to youth:

☐ Provide child care for all church activities.

☐ Make sure the nursery is clean, bright, and easily accessible.

☐ Establish a mentor program for youth. Provide pre-baptismal classes for parents.

☐ Offer peer ministry training for youth and adults to increase communication skills.

☐ Provide devotional materials for families.

☐ Provide opportunities for youth to serve in worship.

☐ Hire a youth and family ministries director.

☐ Create intergenerational events.

☐ Have children and youth complete spiritual-gift inventories.

☐ Have a youth design a congregational Web site.

☐ Offer family-centered first communion classes.

From *Take It to Heart*, pp. 40–42.

Resources to Study for Outreach to Youth

Roehlkepartain, Eugene C., *Building Assets in Congregations: A Practical Guide for Helping Youth Grow Up Healthy*, Search Institute, 1998.

Dumke, Miriam Campbell, *Take It to Heart: An Asset-Based Guide to Nurturing Children, Youth, and Families in Faith Community*, Evangelical Lutheran Church in America and Lutheran Brotherhood, 1998.

Veerman, David R., *Small-Group Ministry with Youth*, Victor Books, 1992.

HEALTH

DESIGN

STUDY

PLAN

ACT

TEND

KNOWING OUR AUDIENCE

VISION TEAM: Challenges arise when implementing new mission strategies. One cause is that many congregations fail to relate to the newer styles of communication that exist today and the different ways in which people receive, process, and assimilate information. The discussion sheet (on the following page) is designed to challenge various groups in your congregation to think beyond their own experiences in ministry and include newer methods of communication and program presentation. Existing, traditional ministries may need to be adapted or replaced to be faithful to God's mission and the congregation's new vision for ministry. Understanding why change is necessary helps the overall process of change and reduces some anxiety.

> **Items to have when using the following discussion sheet**
>
> ☐ Mission and vision statements
>
> ☐ Internal and external demographics in presentation form (graphs, charts, statistics, etc.)
>
> ☐ Charts of current congregational ministries and whom they reach
>
> ☐ Additional resources (see suggestions on this page).
>
> ☐ Details on new mission strategies being implemented

Resources for Further Study on Communication Methods

"Building a Church for New Generations," a four-day conference each spring offered by Community Church of Joy Leadership Center, Glendale, Ariz. (602) 561-0500.

Conferences on reaching unchurched Boomers are held each year at Willow Creek Community Church, P.O. Box 3188, South Barrington, Ill. 60011-3188. Contact them to be placed on mailing list for future seminar registration.

Go Public: Developing Your Plan for Communication Evangelism: A Guide for Congregations. Includes helps to match the correct communication method with the audience you want to reach. Augsburg Fortress (800) 328-4648.

Go Public! Motivating Your Congregation for Communication Evangelism: An Interactive Video Workshop. Augsburg Fortress.

Go Public! Designing Radio Ministry for Communication Evangelism: Models for Audio Outreach. A compact disc and audiocassette include information to create your own radio ministry. Augsburg Fortress.

Postmoderns: The Beliefs, Hopes, and Fears of Young Americans (1965–1981), Craig Kennet Miller. Discipleship Resources, Nashville, Tenn., 1996.

Resources on millennials: Contact Discipleship Resources, (800) 685-4370.

The Telling Congregation: Assessing Your Congregation's Communication Evangelism, 12-page guide. ELCA, 1997. Call (800) 328-4648 to order.

Three Generations: Riding the Waves of Change in Your Church, Gary L. McIntosh, Fleming H. Revell, 1995.

Shifts in Communication Styles

"In just half a normal lifetime, we have gone from a nation unable to link up a coast-to-coast television broadcast, to a world in which current estimates are that more than 80 million people are connected to each other by the Internet and through satellites. Without us being fully aware, the information and technology revolution has reshaped the ways in which many of us learn, work, play, communicate, and think."

—Jim Petersen, *Great Commission Congregations* newsletter, Spring 1999, Division for Congregation Ministries, ELCA

Shift Category	Recent Past	Present & Future
STYLE OF THINKING/DOING	Linear, literate, logical	Multimedia, multisensory, multiprocessing
PROBLEM-SOLVING STYLE	Study, reason, build solutions	Become aware, seek input, network for solutions
NEEDS	Time to study, think, build, and implement	Immediate and just in time
INTERACTION STYLE	Person-to-person, face-to-face	Person-to-person enhanced by computer/technology based
TEACHING/LEARNING MODELS	Workshops, seminars, print, on-site schools	All available options plus Web mentoring, audio CD, telephone mentoring, video workshops, video conferencing, satellite schools, Internet courses

Points to Ponder

- This shift appears to be most rapid in the younger population.
- Groups in the older populations are shifting more gradually.
- Learning is becoming a hands-on activity.
- Effective instructors move past the label of "lack of attention span" to multisensory, multimedia experiences as teaching tools.
- Today, problems are immediate and we don't have time to solve them on our own: Network!

Generational Groupings

GENERATION	BORN	MAIN COMMUNICATION INFLUENCES
Builders	1930–1945	Radio (younger), print (older)
Boomers	1946–1964	TV, professional computers, movies
Generation X	1965–1981	TV, movies, personal computers, video games
Millennials	1982–1999	TV, video, movies, Internet

From "Post-Literate Generations Thrive on Multi-Sensory Learning," Jim Petersen, *Great Commission Congregations* newsletter, Spring 1999, Division for Congregational Ministries, ELCA, and *Now Is the Time*, Craig Kennet Miller and Mary Jane Pierce Norton, Discipleship Resources, 1999.

Discussion questions

- What generations are present in our congregation?
- How does the shift in communication styles affect these groups?
- What evidence is there that present congregational programs need to include newer communication methods?
- What audiences are in our community? How are we attempting to reach them?
- How do these shifts affect the way volunteers operate in our congregation and community?
- How do these shifts affect worship? Christian education? Evangelism? Stewardship?
- When presenting our mission and vision, how might we best communicate to those in our congregation? Community?

MANAGING CONFLICT IN A TURN-AROUND CONGREGATION

LEADERSHIP TEAM: Read Chapter 9, "Overcoming Obstacles," in *Catching the Next Wave* before using this model. Also, refer to the checklist in this workbook entitled, "Dealing with Change in Any Phase" (p. 39).

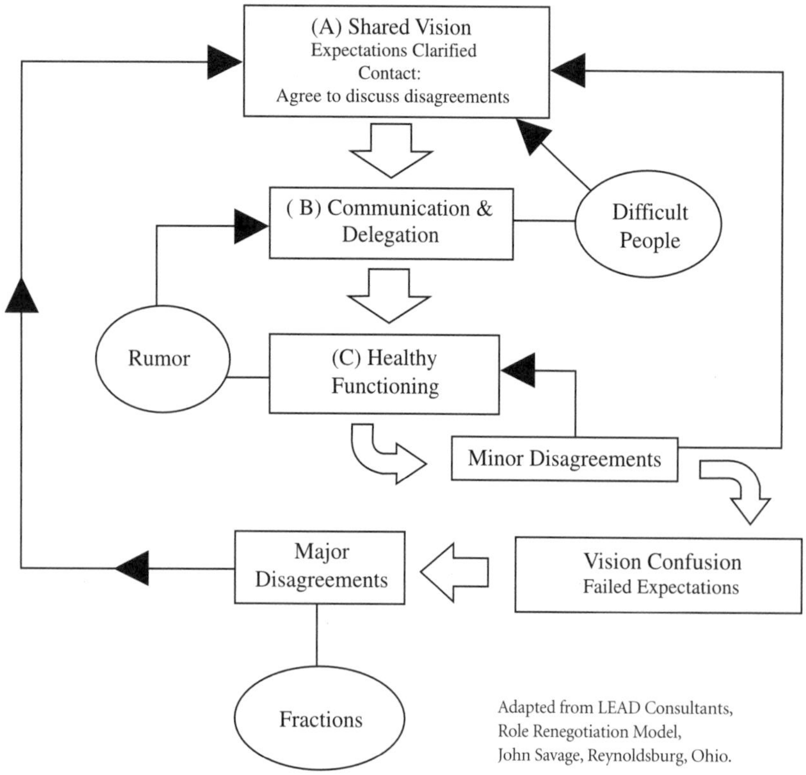

Adapted from LEAD Consultants,
Role Renegotiation Model,
John Savage, Reynoldsburg, Ohio.

Movement of Model

Although factions, rumor, and difficult people can surface at any time in a turn-around experience, the model on this page indicates specific points in the process due to the basic nature of the identified conflict.

DIFFICULT PEOPLE
The delegation of tasks produces power struggles and discontent. Discuss, clarify, and resolve in love.

RUMOR
Making information readily available reduces the opportunities for rumors to even begin. Increase communication of information to reduce rumor.

MINOR DISAGREEMENTS:
Disagreements can be dealt with by immediate attention and adaptation or by discussion and reclarification of expectations. If left unattended, minor disagreements turn into failed expectations and major disagreements develop.

FACTIONS
Major disagreements develop, and when left unattended, people begin to disconnect or leave the congregation, publicly or silently. Address factions immediately: Discuss, clarify, and resolve in love.

Leadership Team Checklist for Using This Model

- Conflict is normal, natural, neutral, narrow, and mutual, and it will occur. The best way to handle this fact is to transform the negative effects of conflict into positive energy and momentum.
- Recognize the three main obstacles to a turn-around congregation: factions, rumor, and difficult people. Study how best to deal with each category (*Catching the Next Wave*, pp. 112–118).
- The diagram on this page illustrates a way to address conflicts as they arise through the advance planning of a contract between all participants. All parties involved "agree to discuss disagreements" and reclarify expectations when questions and concerns arise.

Methods to Assist in Reclarification of Expectations

☐ Use every opportunity to pray together for guidance and strength when conflict arises.

☐ Personal, one-on-one conversation between staff, leaders, and members is effective in handling minor disagreements.

☐ Schedule separate meetings or forums at regular intervals to specifically check progress, discuss tensions, and clarify expectations. Do this in an ongoing manner to help maintain communication and provide nonthreatening opportunities to discuss rumors and minor disagreements. Groupings should include leaders and members and should be open to anyone wanting to participate.

☐ Listen with care and patience to difficult people, but do not lose sight of the mission and vision.

☐ Provide "Caring through Sharing" forms/cards for people to affirm both what is working and what is not working in the turn-around process. The vision team or the governing board shares these in a monthly newsletter to maximize communication.

☐ Use every opportunity, written and verbal, to restate the new congregational vision for ministry and the mission strategies chosen to make that vision happen.

☐ To assist members with conflict resolution, conduct Bible studies on this topic. (See Bible study in this workbook entitled "Managing Conflict Constructively," p. 76.)

☐ If major disagreements develop and are not resolved by reclarifying expectations, consider using the assessment tools entitled "Can This Congregation Turn Around?" and/or "Assessing the Level of Conflict." Seek outside assistance, if necessary.

☐ People may choose to disagree no matter what effort is attempted to reclarify expectations. Recognize that one congregation cannot please everyone. Celebrate your time together and graciously allow those unwilling to support the congregational vision for ministry find a new church home.

☐ Offer prayers of thanksgiving and praise at all times in this process. The Great Commission tells us to "remember, I am with you always, to the end of the age" (Matthew 28:20b). We do not walk alone! Amen!

Resources for Further Study

Diehm, William J., *Caring Criticism*, Stephen Ministries, 1998.

Fischer, Thomas F., Ministry Health Web site: http://genesis.acu.edu/ministry/health or tfischer@journey.com

Haugk, Kenneth C., *Antagonists in the Church*, Augsburg Publishing House, 1988.

Haugk, Kenneth C. and Perry, R. Scott, *Antagonists in the Church Study Guide*, Augsburg Publishing House, 1988.

Koch, Ruth N. and Haugk, Kenneth C., *Speaking the Truth in Love*, Stephen Ministries, 1992.

Richardson, Ronald W., *Creating a Healthier Church*, Fortress Press, 1996.

Savage, John S., *Congregational Corporate Pain* (audiocassette), LEAD Consultants, (614) 864-0156 or leadinc@leadinc.com

Savage, John S., *Role Renegotiation Model* (audiocassette), LEAD Consultants, (614) 864-0156 or leadinc@leadinc.com

---

CARING THROUGH SHARING
Community Church

I affirm the following in our church:

I dislike the following in our church:

My question is:

Name: Date:

(*Anonymous submissions will not be acknowledged.*)

HEALTH
DESIGN
STUDY
PLAN
ACT
TEND

TENDING OUR MISSION STRATEGY

By now you realize that the turn-around process is ongoing. It is also a process where one phase overlaps another as you move forward with your plans for health expressed in your new congregational vision for ministry. Move forward always *integrating* your new vision, *eliminating* or adapting that which doesn't work, *evaluating* the response to the strategies, and *celebrating* your new congregational image. The form on the following page provides check points to keep you focused on the vision and accountable to the process. Below are examples to help you begin.

> Checkpoints keep you *focused* on the vision and *accountable* to the process.

Mission Strategy

Provide welcoming hospitality in worship.

Goals and Objectives

1. Members recognize guests.
   - ☐ Establish a greeting team at the main entrance to our church.
   - ☐ Provide coffee fellowship.
   - ☐ Provide friendship registers.

2. Provide guest-friendly worship bulletins.
   - ☐ Obtain appropriate copyrights to reproduce the service in the weekly bulletin.
   - ☐ Reduce the amount of inserts and condense announcements.
   - ☐ Upgrade the software used to produce our worship bulletin.

3. Update our facility for guest comfort.
   - ☐ Add directional signs to the nursery and rest rooms.
   - ☐ Mark five parking spaces for visitor use.
   - ☐ Provide an information center with a person to answer questions.

Tending the Mission Strategy

MISSION STRATEGY: Provide welcoming hospitality in worship.

GOAL ASSIGNED: Members recognize guests.

REPORT ON OBJECTIVE: Establish a greeting team at the main entrance to our church.

REVIEW DATE	INTEGRATE	ELIMINATE	EVALUATE	CELEBRATE
1. Three months from start	1. Recruiting of team completed by personal invitations	1. Found that one training date for all didn't work; training individually	1. —	1. —
2. Three months from last check	2. Reason for team announced in weekly bulletin and newsletter	2. —	2. Members and guests receptive to greeter	2. Thanked new team in newsletter and bulletin
3. Break in church calendar	3. Break in church calendar	3. Break in church calendar	3. Break in church calendar	3.
4. Three months from end of break	4. Established schedule for next six months	4. Keep training; added name tags for greeters	4. Name tags a big plus!	4. Working so well new people have volunteered to greet.

Mission Strategy Report Form

Governing Board Checklist

- [ ] Pray for guidance and faithfulness.
- [ ] How will we involve the congregation in the evaluation process?
- [ ] How will we inform the congregation of the progress being made?
- [ ] How will we support and communicate with the groups assigned these tasks?
- [ ] How will we verify the faithfulness of the progress in our tasks with the congregational mission and vision?
- [ ] Offer prayers of thanksgiving and begin the checklist again!

MISSION STRATEGY: _____

_____

GOAL ASSIGNED: _____

_____

OBJECTIVE: _____

_____

TASK FORCE LEADER: _____

_____

Review date	Integrate	Eliminate	Evaluate	Celebrate
1.	1.	1.	1.	1.
2.	2.	2.	2.	2.
3.	3.	3.	3.	3.
4.	4.	4.	4.	4.

HEALTH

DESIGN

STUDY

PLAN

ACT

TEND

Biblical Reflection
1 MANAGING CONFLICT CONSTRUCTIVELY

Opening Question:

How do you usually handle personal conflicts?

Opening Prayer

Almighty God, we gather in your presence to grow stronger in our service to you. Guide us this day to be positive, constructive seekers of your will. Amen.

Reflection Scripture

James 4:1

Setting of Scripture

The New Testament book of James is believed by some scholars to have been written by the oldest brother of Jesus, James. Early on, James did not believe that Jesus was the Messiah, but later became a prominent church leader of the Jerusalem council. In this letter, James addresses Jewish Christians struggling with poverty and oppression. These and other social tensions finally led to the Judean war of A.D. 66–70. James encourages the taming of the tongue, faith and good deeds, patience in suffering, and that everyone "be quick to listen, slow to speak, and slow to anger" (James 1:19).

Points to Ponder

- Factions are a serious threat to church health. Factions grow when there is little direct communication between constituencies. Healing occurs when members of each constituency sit and listen to one another (p. 113).

- Just as physical pain alerts us to problems within our bodies, so too does internal conflict focus attention on what really matters: the coming kingdom of Christ (p. 119).

- Growing in one's understanding of, and reactions to, conflict not only prepares strong congregational leaders but benefits the personal lives of the leaders as well (p. 112).

(From *Catching the Next Wave*.)

Exploring Scriptures

What do we learn about managing conflict from these scriptures?

- Ephesians 4:15, 25–26

- Ephesians 4:29–32

- Romans 14:19

- Philippians 2:4

- Philippians 2:5–11

Discussion Questions

☐ What issues in the past created division in the congregation, and how was it handled?

☐ How does our congregation deal with new ideas for ministry?

☐ How might we encourage peaceful and constructive dialog amidst inevitable tension and disagreement? (1 Peter 5:8)

☐ How might congregational leaders help prevent conflicts in the congregation?

Summary Questions

"Conflict is not simply a reality for the plateaued or declining congregation but for the turn-around congregation as well" (*Catching the Next Wave*, p. 108). What does this statement mean for your congregation? How might your congregation improve its skills in managing conflict?

Closing Prayer

Lord and Giver of life, we acknowledge our selfish nature and look to you for the strength needed to be faithful to our calling as disciples. Create in each of us the vision to work together as a healthy, living body, praising and growing your kingdom. In the name of Jesus, we pray. Amen.

Biblical Reflection

2 PRAYER

Opening Question:

When has prayer been an instrument of strength or comfort in your life?

Opening Prayer

Lord, it is so good to be able to talk with you! Thank you for this day and for this time together. May we grow in strength of faith and serve you with joyful hearts. Amen.

Reflection Scripture

Romans 8:26-29

Setting of Scripture

Paul wrote this essay-style letter to the Christians in the city of Rome. He wrote to prepare them for his visit and to present the basic message of salvation to those who had not yet heard these teachings from an apostle. This letter also encourages the church to live its Christian faith in practical ways. In Romans 8:26-29, Paul tells the people that the spirit supports us in our weakness by helping us know what to pray (v. 26). The Holy Spirit intercedes on our behalf with sincerity and feeling (v. 26) and God hears what is in our hearts more accurately than we could explain in words (v. 27). In verses 28 and 29 we hear that prayer is answered according to the will of God, not our own will. Paul's counsel to the Romans on prayer is still helpful to us today!

Points to Ponder

- "But when we pray, genuinely pray, the real condition of our heart is revealed: This is as it should be. This is when God truly begins to work with us. The adventure is just beginning" (*Prayer*, Richard Foster, p. 11).

- "Someone has said that when we work, we work; but when we pray, *God* works" (*Too Busy Not to Pray*, Bill Hybels, p. 11).

- Air is to our bodies what prayer is to our souls (adapted from *Prayer*, O. Hallesby).

Exploring Scriptures

What do we learn about prayer from these scriptures?

- Psalm 66:18
- James 4:3
- Philippians 4:6
- Luke 11:9
- Colossians 1:9-10
- Ephesians 5:17

Discussion Questions

☐ What does my personal prayer life look like? How might it be strengthened?

☐ What does our congregation do to encourage both personal and corporate prayer?

☐ How might our congregation encourage prayer during the turn-around process?

☐ Bill Hybels defines God's answers to prayer in the following four ways:

1. No. Your request is not in God's will.

2. Slow. Your request is not God's will at this time.

3. Grow. Your motives are wrong.

4. Go. Your request, timing, and spiritual condition are okay—Yes!

(*Leading Life-Changing Small Groups*; Bill Donohue, Zondervan, 1996.)

How might this help your understanding of answered prayer?

Summary Question

"Prayer is both a tool and a gift from God." What might this statement mean to our congregation?

Closing Prayer

Gracious God, our time with you is often spent by us being distracted and shortened by busy schedules. Give us the strength to resist the temptations that keep us from spending time with you. We pray this in the name of Jesus. Amen.

HEALTH
DESIGN
STUDY
PLAN
ACT
TEND

HEALTH
DESIGN
STUDY
PLAN
ACT
TEND

Biblical Reflection

3 GROWING IS OF GOD

Opening Question:

What experiences, events, or people have influenced your faith journey?

Opening Prayer

Lord God, we gather to grow closer to you, and through serving you, to grow your church, the body of Christ. Honor us with your presence and guide us in your ways. Open our hearts and minds to hear and see what tasks we are called to complete even if it means to change the way we do ministry. In Jesus' name we pray. Amen.

Reflection Scripture:

1 Corinthians 3:6-7

Setting of Scripture

At the time Paul wrote this letter to the church at Corinth, the conduct of the people had strayed from the teachings of Christ. Disagreements, greed, hatred, envy, marital difficulties, and sexual immorality were common. In addition to these inappropriate behaviors, factions had formed because people were pledging allegiance to individual church leaders who had led them to Christ. Paul is clear that Christian leaders are *servants* of God, and that although all are called to share the good news, the foundation on which to build the church is Christ Jesus. God alone makes things grow (v. 7).

Points to Ponder

- Health is the dynamic interplay of wondrous layers of interrelationship to accomplish God's purpose and glory (p. 3).

- Especially in the 20th century, pluralism and laxity have taken their toll on the growth of the Christian faith in Europe and North America. At the same time, the church in Africa and Asia has grown remarkably! (p. 7).

- God has chosen to use us as workers in the garden of life (p. 8).

(From *Catching the Next Wave*.)

Exploring Scriptures

What do we learn about growth from these scriptures?

- Genesis 1:1

- 1 Corinthians 12:1-20

- 2 Peter 3:18

- Matthew 28:19-20

- Acts 1:8

Discussion Questions

☐ What opportunities in our congregation help participants to grow in their faith?

☐ What activities provide an open invitation and anticipate that new people will attend?

☐ How are people encouraged to use their spiritual gifts?

☐ Does the structure of our congregation support *mission* (reaching new people) or *maintenance* (focus on membership and status quo)?

Summary Question

The Church Membership Initiative (Aid Association for Lutherans, 1993) discovered that "congregations that want to grow, might grow"(p. 7).

What does this mean for our congregation?

Closing Prayer

Together, Lord, we hear your message, we seek your will, and we serve only you. Allow us to honor you in all that we say and do. In Jesus' name we pray. Amen.

Biblical Reflection
4 TEAMWORK PROMOTES HEALTH

HEALTH
DESIGN
STUDY
PLAN
ACT
TEND

Opening Question:

When you exchange gifts with another person, what are the usual reactions of both parties?

Opening Prayer

Gracious God, you have given each of us many gifts, gifts that we can share with others. Bless our time together now, that we might learn more about how to bring unity to your church, the body of Christ, by sharing our gifts in partnership with one another. Amen.

Reflection Scripture

Ephesians 4:11–6

Setting of Scripture

The apostle Paul is writing to the Christians in Ephesus. Unlike many of his other letters to churches, Paul does not focus on a particular heresy, but on helping the people understand to the fullest God's love, grace, and intent for the church. Practical helps for living a daily life to the glory of God include understanding that God gave each of us differing gifts to minister to one another and to use to grow the body of Christ, the church. Those called as leaders develop more leaders, and through prayer and working together as the body of Christ, move God's plan of unity and maturity for the church towards fulfillment.

Points to Ponder

- Lutheran pastor and church consultant Peter Steinke defines *health* as wholeness—all parts working together to maintain balance and interacting to function as a whole. Health is a continuous process, the ongoing interplay of multiple forces and conditions. (*Healthy Congregations: A Systems Approach*, p. vii).

- An essential feature of vital, energetic congregations is how they manage the inevitable conflict that comes with change and people living in community (p. 10).

- The healthy congregation as a living entity must also adapt to its context in order to retain its relevance (p. 10).

(From *Catching the Next Wave*.)

Exploring Scriptures

What do we learn about team work from these scriptures?

- 1 Corinthians 12:12-20
- Romans 12:4-5
- 1 Peter 4:10

Discussion Questions

- [ ] What main categories of groups exist in our congregation?
- [ ] How do groups in our congregation interact?

- [ ] Are cooperation and encouragement personality traits of these groups, or are conflict and power struggles more evident?

- [ ] Do groups give up on projects or do they rally in crisis?

- [ ] Does our congregation develop working ministries or try to resurrect, nonproductive programs? For example: events where attendance is consistently low, programs that attempt to reach an age group no longer present in the congregation or community, small groups that meet needs not required by the community, activities that use old learning styles and dated printed materials, programs that are established to support the statement, "we've always done it that way."

Summary Question

Is team work a characteristic of our congregation?

Closing Prayer

Thank you, Lord, for this time together. We thank you for your presence among us and for the ability to grow by better understanding ourselves and our congregation. We ask that you continue to guide us as we learn to work together to build your church. In Jesus' name we pray. Amen.

HEALTH
DESIGN
STUDY
PLAN
ACT
TEND

5 Biblical Reflection VISION

Opening Question:

Describe a project that never was completed because you didn't know how to accomplish the goal.

Opening Prayer

Gracious God, we thank you for this day and for this time together to grow in our understanding of mission and vision. Keep us mindful of our task and open to your message. We pray in the name of Jesus who, knowing your mission and vision, died that we might have eternal life. Amen.

Reflection Scripture

Luke 9:22 and Mark 10:32-34

Setting of Scripture

Throughout the Gospel accounts of the life of Jesus, we hear the mission and vision that God called Jesus to accomplish. God's mission as stated by Jesus to one of the crowds who followed him was, "I must proclaim the good news of the kingdom of God to the other cities also; for I was sent for this purpose" (Luke 4:43). This mission was continued past his earthly life when he commissioned the apostles to "go therefore and make disciples" (Matthew 28:19-20). Jesus' vision was just as clear. He was to die on the cross and rise three days later. This specific act supported God's mission.

Points to Ponder

Review Chapters 4 and 6 in *Catching the Next Wave.*

■ Only a vivid mental picture of the future God desires, shared among the majority of the membership, will propel the congregation through its status quo. No single program or quick fix will suffice (p. 71).

■ A shared vision is a deliberate, collective listening to God's guidance toward the future (p. 71).

■ God will be the author of this foundational vision for mission, for only God can transform the deepest core of the membership's unexpressed dreams for its future and align human will with God's divine will" (p. 73).

(From *Catching the Next Wave.*)

Exploring Scriptures

What do we learn about vision from these scriptures?

■ Acts 5:38

■ Isaiah 55:8

■ Habakkuk 2:2–3

■ 1 Corinthians 12:12

Discussion Questions

☐ How does our congregation plan for the future?

☐ Do groups within the congregation work together? Why or why not?

☐ What visions for ministry exist within the congregation now?

☐ Is (are) the existing vision(s) now operating within our congregation supporting God's mission to "make disciples"? Why or why not?

Summary Question

"The old Adam inside us all is far too attached to absolute security and predictability. God, in contrast, leads us to the edge asking us to completely trust" (*Catching the Next Wave*, p. 78).

What might this statement mean to our congregation?

Closing Prayer

Guide us safely home, dear Lord, and grant us time to reflect on our dedication to serving you. Keep us strong and focused on determining your vision for our congregation. In the name of Jesus, we pray. Amen.